SECRETS OF A DIVORCE LAWYER

Testimonials

For many people, reaching out for legal help and working with a lawyer can be daunting at the best of times, especially when you need help because of a relationship breakdown. Many people, including family and friends, have their own opinions about how the legal system works and what you should do. Unfortunately, the reality is that many of the well-intended suggestions, tips and advice are not helpful and can lead to disaster!

As such, it is extremely refreshing to have a book that gives simple and accurate information about what to do and expect. This book provides a simple ABC template to help you get the right legal help for you.

Zita Ngor – Chief Executive, Women's Legal Service (SA)

Secrets of a Divorce Lawyer is well written and jam packed with sound and practical tips that help the reader navigate every step of the Family Law labyrinth and save some money to boot. Every separated person should read this book.

Brian McQuade – Family Law Barrister

Shaya's book cuts through the 'legalese' that often bamboozles separated people who are already experiencing the often-overwhelming emotions associated with separation. Clear, concise and easy to read, Shaya's book is the ideal 'how-to' guide for dealing with the necessary legalities in a quick and relatively pain-free manner.

Olivia Kay – Family Consultant & Family Law Court Report writer

Shaya has taken the often complex and scary world of Family Law and used her highly respected experience to arm people with the necessary information and confidence needed to navigate the process and understand their options. *Secrets of a Divorce Lawyer* properly and helpfully shares the tips and tricks separating families should be aware of in simple and clear language that is encouraging, realistic and (most importantly) easy to understand.

Kirsten Poetsch – Principal Solicitor, Community Justice Centres SA

Everyone who is even considering separating or knows someone who is going through separation should start with this book. Shaya has written a user-friendly, no-jargon guide to the challenges of separation and divorce. At a time when everything seems overwhelming, this book will be the light to guide you in a tough time.

Roxanne Nathan – Family Dispute Resolution Practitioner & Child Consultant

Provocative for the profession. Hugely practical. A wonderful resource.

Vanessa Lindsay – Family Law Barrister

This book shines a torch on what can be one of the darkest and most confusing times in a person's life. It offers sensible advice to help navigate separation and guides you through the complexities of Family Law.

Dora Fuda – Barrister & Accredited Mediator

Shaya has taken her years of experience and condensed her knowledge into an easy-to-read, go-to guide for anyone going through the Family Law system. The book is filled with practical tips for getting through the Family Law process in the best way possible. There are particular gems scattered throughout the book that make it evident that Shaya has taken the time to really listen to her clients as she promotes ways to assist people with empathy through the difficult process of separation. A must-read for anyone embarking on this journey.

Suzie Derewlany – Family Law Solicitor & Independent Children's Lawyer

What a great book! As a Family Law barrister, I can say that this is a book that is necessary and should be read as a textbook guide to navigating Family Law issues, particularly litigation.

It is detailed and written with thoughtfulness and sensitivity. I recommend it to all those interested and involved in sorting out their parental and property issues.

Rose-Marie Read – Family Law Barrister

Secrets of a Divorce Lawyer is an outstanding book and an essential read for anyone experiencing or contemplating separation.

With clear explanations of the legal process, cost-saving ideas, common pitfalls and misconceptions to look out for – all written in plain English – this book will empower you to have more control over your separation. It is possible to reduce the high levels of both stress and legal fees commonly associated with Family Law matters and this book does an excellent job of explaining how.

In addition, I would highly recommend this book as an important resource for students studying Family Law or the Graduate Diploma in Family Dispute Resolution. The insider's view by an experienced family lawyer is both informative and entertaining.

Michelle Ford – Senior Coordinator Family Law Pathways

Secrets of a Divorce Lawyer can easily be subtitled 'Empowerment'. It does not profess to be a detailed guide to Family Law, but for those who find themselves about to be (or recently) separated, it will be an invaluable tool to assist them in navigating the complexities of the Family Law system, in taking ownership of their case and in making informed decisions.

Unlike so many self-help documents, it does not just focus on the legalities. Shaya Lewis-Dermody has 'opened up' the system to help people who are separating do so much themselves before seeing a lawyer so they can reduce the work their lawyer will have to do (and the associated costs). Importantly, however, the author does not seek to remove the lawyer from the system entirely; each separation is unique and still requires expert analysis, advice and action.

Secrets of a Divorce Lawyer is also an invaluable book for students undertaking placements at university-run legal advice services, providing an overview of the areas of Family Law that need to be considered when providing preliminary advice and subsequent referral to an experienced Family Law practitioner. It is also an excellent bridge between the more theoretical aspects taught in Family Law and the realities of separation.

Dr Ross Savvas – Adelaide Law School Clinics
University of Adelaide

Secrets of a Divorce Lawyer
Copyright © 2021 by Shaya Lewis.
All rights reserved.

Published by Grammar Factory Publishing, an imprint of MacMillan Company Limited.

No part of this book may be used or reproduced in any manner whatsoever without the prior written permission of the author, except in the case of brief passages quoted in a book review or article. All enquiries should be made to the author.

Grammar Factory Publishing
MacMillan Company Limited
25 Telegram Mews, 39th Floor, Suite 3906
Toronto, Ontario, Canada
M5V 3Z1

www.grammarfactory.com

Lewis, Shaya, 1979–
 Secrets of a Divorce Lawyer: An insider's guide for successfully navigating separation and saving on legal fees / Shaya Lewis.

Paperback ISBN 978-198973-737-8
eBook ISBN 978-198973-736-1

 1. LAW038020 LAW / Family Law / Divorce & Separation 2. LAW038000 LAW / Family Law / General 3. FAM015000 FAMILY & RELATIONSHIPS / Divorce & Separation.

Production Credits
Cover design by Designerbility.
Interior layout design by Dania Zafar.
Book production and editorial services by Grammar Factory Publishing.

Grammar Factory's Carbon Neutral Publishing Commitment
From January 1st, 2020 onwards, Grammar Factory Publishing is proud to be neutralizing the carbon footprint of all printed copies of its authors' books printed by or ordered directly through Grammar Factory or its affiliated companies through the purchase of Gold Standard-Certified International Offsets.

Disclaimer
The material in this publication is of the nature of general comment only and does not represent professional advice. It is not intended to provide specific guidance for particular circumstances, and it should not be relied on as the basis for any decision to take action or not take action on any matter which it covers. Readers should obtain professional advice where appropriate, before making any such decision. To the maximum extent permitted by law, the author and publisher disclaim all responsibility and liability to any person, arising directly or indirectly from any person taking or not taking action based on the information in this publication.

SECRETS OF A DIVORCE LAWYER

Tips for successfully navigating your separation and saving on legal fees

SHAYA LEWIS-DERMODY

'Today you are You, that is truer than true. There is no one alive who is Youer than You.'

– Dr Seuss

[Every matter is different!]

CAVEAT

As all lawyers do, I start the book with a standard 'caveat'. The contents of this book are not intended as legal advice, as every matter is unique. The book is of a general nature. When I make reference to legislation throughout the book, I am referring to the *Family Law Act 1975* (*Cth*). The legislation is applicable Australia wide, though Western Australia has its own Family Law Court system and legislation. The principles found in this book are generally applicable Australia wide.

This book is not intended to be a substitute for professional legal advice.

GUIDE TO LEGAL TERMS

I have included a guide to legal terms at the end of this book for your reference. The guide provides some definitions of commonly used legal terms. I have tried my best to avoid 'legalese' throughout this book!

READERSHIP

This book presumes that you have already separated. If you are considering separation, then I suggest you reach out and get some personal or relationship counselling and also specific legal advice *prior* to separation.

If you have not yet separated, then you are in a much better position than most. The first thing to determine is whether you want to proceed with the separation or if there is scope to work on the relationship and engage in relationship counselling. If you are unsure, then it is still worthwhile reading through this book so that you can be well prepared if you do ultimately separate.

Contents

Introduction: 'I Did Not Plan To Be Here' 1

PART ONE: WHERE TO START 13
Chapter 1: Everyone has a Family Law story 15
Chapter 2: What are *your* needs? An overview of Family Law issues 17
Chapter 3: Immediate tips post separation 21
Chapter 4: Taking back control 27

PART TWO: LAWYERS 45
Chapter 5: Finding a lawyer 47
Chapter 6: Free legal advice & representation 53
Chapter 7: Your first meeting with a lawyer 65
Chapter 8: Communications with a lawyer 71
Chapter 9: How to choose a lawyer (if you decide to get one) 75
Chapter 10: Paying your lawyer 79
Chapter 11: Unbundled legal services 87
Chapter 12: Getting the most out of your lawyer 91
Chapter 13: Ditching your lawyer! 99
Chapter 14: Dealing with your ex-partner's lawyer 107

PART THREE: DIVORCE 113
Chapter 15: DIY divorce 115
Chapter 16: Divorce applications 119

PART FOUR: PROPERTY 125
Chapter 17: Property matters 127

Chapter 18: Property settlement – the four-step process	135
Chapter 19: Valuing the property pool	145
Chapter 20: Property division – urgent matters	155
Chapter 21: Ways to resolve your property matter	163
Chapter 22: Agreement reached?	171

PART FIVE: CHILDREN — 183

Chapter 23: Parenting matters	185
Chapter 24: Formalising parenting matters	203
Chapter 25: Child support	213

PART SIX: COURT — 217

Chapter 26: Initiating court proceedings	219
Chapter 27: Going to court	223
Bonus Tips	242
Final Thoughts	250
Caveat	252
Helpful resources	253
Glossary: Guide to legal terms	256
Acknowledgements	266
About the author	267

Introduction:
'I Did Not Plan To Be Here'

Nobody goes into a relationship planning to break up!

You're likely reading this book because you have separated from your partner and, when it comes to the legal issues, you either do not know where to start or are trying to navigate our complex and stressful Family Law jurisdiction.

Most people who have separated simply do not know where to start.

You're in a good place.

You did not plan to be here. We plan for our wedding for months and even years! But when it comes to separation and divorce, it is very common for us to be unprepared, often due to the stress and other emotions, such as anxiety, grief and overwhelm.

This applies whether a wedding has taken place or not.

The most recent data from the Australian Bureau of Statistics, released in late 2020, indicates that in 2019 there were around

114,000 marriages registered and 49,000 divorces granted. A decrease in the number of marriages registered in recent years is likely due to more couples living in de facto relationships.

The Australian Institute of Family Studies reported in 2020 that cohabitation without the intention to marry has become increasingly accepted, as most of us are aware anecdotally. It's important to know that even if you were not married or did not formally register your relationship, if you were in a de facto relationship, then you are likely to have similar rights and protection under the *Family Law Act*, which came into operation in 1976.

The cost of separation

Did you know that separation and divorce can cost more than a wedding? According to *moneysmart.gov.au*, the average Australian wedding costs $36,000. It is not uncommon for legal fees to exceed that amount – particularly with litigious matters that end up in the court system.

Whether you are coming out of a married or de facto relationship, you may be feeling stressed about how you are either going to pay to fight for the custody or safety of your children or navigate your property settlement negotiations. It can be even more challenging if your ex-partner has a lawyer and you simply don't know where to start.

Many people presume that if you cannot afford to pay a lawyer, you will be provided one by your state Legal Aid office. That is not correct. Funding is limited by guidelines around means and merit for parenting matters, and there are only very limited matters that are funded to help you negotiate your property division.

But you should not feel disheartened if you cannot afford a lawyer.

If you do engage a lawyer, then this book is armed with tips to potentially save you thousands in legal fees.

If you go it alone without a lawyer, then this book will assist you with practical and money-saving tips while self-representing.

Either way, it will also arm you with knowledge and some peace of mind.

Why this book?

There are already publications and resources around self-care in Family Law. In fact, I wrote the book *Separate Ways: Surviving Post-Separation Grief, the Stress of Divorce or Separation, and the Family Law Process* to focus on the stress, grief and loss that you are likely to experience following relationship breakdown. Self-care is extremely important and I urge you to find the guidance of a support service or counsellor. If you do not know where to start, then consult your general practitioner, who can discuss options around a mental health care plan referral.

This book does not focus on self-help. This book is here to provide practical tips to those in the Family Law system to **save you money**. As a lawyer practising in the Family Law jurisdiction for almost twenty years, I have the insider knowledge to empower you to take better control of your current situation and also potentially save you thousands of dollars.

I don't believe in dirty tricks. I also don't believe in keeping them a secret!

I suspect that a number of the legal profession will be critical of this book and many may be unhappy that I am sharing my 'insider tips'! Some may even feel a little uncomfortable and nervous. That's okay and probably an indication that the book is going to be helpful for you – the reader.

But why would I, a lawyer and owner of a law firm, share my insider tips to save you money? Surely that would be taking business and potential earnings away from myself?!

Lawyers have a reputation with the public of overcharging clients while lining their own pockets. Anyone going through a separation is aware of the emotional toll and struggle involved. The additional financial stress when using a divorce lawyer or having your hand forced through the Family Law system can be enough to drive even the strongest person to tipping point.

The truth is that I set up my law firm, The Family Law Project, around ten years ago because, at that time, I recognised a gap in the market – there were very few fixed-fee lawyers. I was also finding more people in the middle-income bracket who did not qualify for legal aid but were unable to afford to pay a traditional law firm. I sought (and continue to seek) to bridge that gap. Many of you are likely to be part of the group that we are now referring to as the 'missing middle'.

The reality is that there is plenty of work to go around among already established law firms. However, my other observation and concern is that there are many people who have separated who do not obtain any legal advice or input during any stage of resolving their property or parenting matter (whether in court or not).

I cannot imagine how difficult it must be for someone in a completely foreign system trying to navigate their way through negotiation, document drafting or even court. Navigating our Family Law system can be difficult at the best of times, let alone when you are dealing with your own matter and your own feelings of stress and perhaps grief and loss following the breakdown of your relationship.

Nobody goes into a relationship expecting to separate! You have likely been thrown into the Family Law system with no legal training and perhaps no previous experience in separation. Even if you have separated previously, each matter is unique and can be settled in various ways. You are not a Family Law expert and it is unlikely that you are a willing participant in this process.

In terms of some cost-saving tips, you are in the right place.

Going it alone

If you're 'going it alone', remember you're not alone!

Let's look at the statistics in terms of self-represented litigants in court.

The most recent Family Law Court's annual report of 2019-2020 shows a small increase in matters involving one or both parties not having legal representation at some stage during court proceedings (twenty-one per cent). The Family Court of Western Australia's (FCWA) 2019 annual review (also the most recent available) shows that of those applying for parenting orders, forty-seven per cent are self-represented; in financial matters, twenty-four per cent are self-represented at some point; and of those applying to the court to formalise their private property agreement, close to forty per cent are self-represented.

Some people are able to resolve their property or parenting matter by agreement and negotiation. There are no actual court proceedings, but the agreement and relevant paperwork are submitted to the court to formalise the agreement.

There are a number of reasons why someone may not engage the assistance of a lawyer. You will have your own unique reason why you navigate some or all of your Family Law journey on a self-represented basis or not.

The Family Law Courts conducted a Satisfaction Survey in 2015 and the most common reason that people gave for not being legally represented during the court proceedings was that they could not afford a lawyer or did not qualify for legal aid. Having said that, some forty-one per cent responded that they had a *preference* for presenting their own case and did not believe a lawyer was necessary. They considered their matter easy or straightforward or had had bad experiences with lawyers in the past.

What was clear in this survey was that the level of income alone was not the sole determinant of whether someone engaged a lawyer for court proceedings. It was also clear that even if a litigant was self-represented in the proceedings, almost seventy per cent had obtained legal advice *at some point*. Some of the feedback was that the legal input was helpful; however, some comments included complaints about lawyers not listening, or being uninterested, expensive or ill prepared.

An earlier study from 2000 found that many litigants who said they did not want or need a lawyer did so because of high levels of distrust of lawyers and the legal profession. I suspect not a lot has changed now... some twenty-plus years later.

My thoughts are that most people who are self-represented at any stage of their separation, trying to navigate negotiation or mediation themselves or ending up as a litigant in person in court, will have difficulties with the process and also lack understanding of the process and the legal jargon used.

The 2015 Family Court report included the following comments about some of the experiences of people who were attending court without a lawyer:

Feel intimidated, court jargon and scared in front of judge.

Technical and traumatic process, so hard being unrepresented doing voluminous paperwork.

Process is quite difficult to understand. Hard to grasp the requirements.

I know that many clients who contact us for the first time early in the separation are experiencing a complete sense of overwhelm and do not know how to proceed. This is more than likely the case for the people who don't end up contacting a lawyer at this stage or at all. So, whether you're going it alone or expecting to seek legal support at some point, this is the book I'd like you to be armed with.

Shark-infested waters

I wish that it were not necessary to write this book. I suspect there will be backlash and that a number of the profession will not appreciate me putting my knowledge to paper.

I would like to say with confidence that the Family Law system is fair and that all family lawyers are going to provide you with reasonable advice and guidance. Unfortunately, that is not always the case. While there are many admirable lawyers, the reality is that the system can still seem dog eat dog. Having worked in the jurisdiction for almost twenty years, I cannot say I have seen it all, but I have certainly seen a *lot*. I have assisted clients through amicable separation agreements all the way to high-conflict matters that reach court and go to trial. A lot of the work that I do is when the court appoints me to act as an independent children's lawyer for children in very high-conflict or difficult matters.

It's really pleasing to see a new age of lawyers now practising in the Family Law space who are focused on client outcomes and alternative dispute resolution or collaborative methods. The reality is, however, that amicable resolutions generally require not only the lawyers but also *both parties* to be focused on those outcomes.

Often, parties who are separating are not on their best behaviour due to the emotion involved and perhaps the circumstances of the separation. Likewise, I have observed a number of lawyers who are not genuine in their attempt to settle a Family Law matter in a way that minimises stress and cost to both parties. I have seen all of the 'dirty lawyer' tricks, including overcharging clients through unnecessary work, 'milking files' to generate fees, participating in last-minute service of documents to put a party at a disadvantage, and drafting unnecessary correspondence or documents in order to generate legal fees.

Working as a lawyer in Sydney, I observed lawyers in the Sydney Registry going straight into the courtroom without even acknowledging or discussing the matter with the opposing lawyer. How can there be a genuine attempt to settle a matter if there is no communication between lawyers?!

I wrote the above paragraph about my experience in Sydney back in 2017 when first jotting down ideas for this book. It turns out that I was not alone in my thinking at that time. Later that year, a Family Court judge, Justice Benjamin, released a judgment in relation to the issue of legal fees spent by parties fighting out parenting and property matters in the Sydney Family Law Court. He referred to the parties having spent an 'eye-watering' combined total of $860,000 in legal fees and disbursements. Eight-hundred and sixty thousand dollars! Regardless of the size of the asset pool to be divided, how can those legal fees be justified? In my view, they can't.

Justice Benjamin referred the matter to the Legal Services Commission of New South Wales and requested that they investigate and consider whether the costing approaches by the respective lawyers could constitute professional misconduct. He also asked that they investigate whether all of the work conducted by the lawyers was *necessary*. In addition, he requested that they consider whether the legal fees were *proportionate*.

Another comment that Justice Benjamin made in this remarkable judgemnt was that he had an increasing concern about the high levels of costs charged, particularly in the Sydney Registry. He said, '*In the Sydney Registry of the Family Court I have observed what seems to be a culture of bitter, adversarial and highly aggressive family law litigation.*' He referred to the high legal costs being '... *destructive of the emotional, social and financial wellbeing of the parties and their children. It must stop.*'

These are very admirable and strong comments from a judicial officer.

If you are reading this book, then I suspect that you do not have a lazy few hundred thousand dollars to spend in legal fees, nor would you consider doing so. The case and the comments by Justice Benjamin are fascinating, though, as it is clear that the Court also has concerns in relation to the legal fees charged by some lawyers.

Another caveat. After all, I am a lawyer! There are many good lawyers – we're not all sharks! My view is that if you can afford to receive legal advice, then you should do so. But I also recognise that not everyone can afford to pay a lawyer on an ongoing basis. This book aims not only to help those who are self-represented but also provide tips and guidance to those who do not want to throw money away on lawyers unnecessarily.

How to use this book

The book is divided into six parts, covering different facets of separation, some of which will apply to you at this point in time and some of which will not be relevant to you at this stage (or at all).

The sections of the book have been divided to cover the following:

- Where to start
- Lawyers
- Divorce
- Property
- Children
- Court

Feel free to read the book from cover to cover. Or you may prefer to dip in and out of the book based on your current personal situation.

I do, however, recommend that you familiarise yourself with the book in its entirety at some stage. For example, if your matter is not currently in court, it is still a good idea to refer to those sections of the book to arm yourself with the knowledge of what to expect in the event that your matter does end up in court (this may also encourage you to stay out of court!).

Likewise, even if you do not envisage that you will engage a lawyer at any stage, it is still going to be helpful for you to familiarise yourself with the information I provide about obtaining legal advice, as it includes information and money-saving tips that you may not have previously turned your mind to.

So, whatever page you're turning to next, let's begin!

PART ONE:
WHERE TO START

Everyone has a Family Law story

EACH AND EVERY FAMILY HAS THEIR OWN SPECIFIC ISSUES when they separate. It seems these days everyone has their own Family Law story and I suspect there is no shortage of advice out there. When you open up about your separation, you are likely to have your hairdresser, your friend, the barista (not barrister!) and whoever else you are willing to listen to reach out to offer you advice based on *their* experience.

My advice as a family lawyer is to listen to anyone with an open mind and seek their emotional support and comfort as opposed to legal advice and guidance. You may want to chat to them about how they found their experience or general procedural and practical information. But just because they were able to agree on a '50/50' division of the assets or the court made an order about shared care, meaning that they have the children for equal weeks, doesn't mean that is the right outcome for your family.

I have listened to so many clients at their initial consultation who presume that there will be '50/50' shared care of the children, or that there will automatically be a division of the assets. This is often based on what their well-meaning friend advised them or what they read on the internet, and it is certainly not the case.

Please also be wary of online forums written by non-lawyers. I have been horrified reading some of the so-called 'advice' on those forums! I understand that people are likely to be well-meaning, but some of the information given is simply inaccurate.

 **Lean on friends and family for emotional support but not for legal advice. It could end up costing you money!**

What are *your* needs? An overview of Family Law issues

EVERY SINGLE PERSON GOING THROUGH FAMILY LAW IS HAVING a different experience. Every family differs. The dynamics of each family, the relationships and the circumstances around separation differ. The assets at separation or arrangements for the children (if any) differ. You may have been married or de facto. It may have been a long or short relationship. There may have been family violence. Every matter has its own complexities. Before getting too far ahead, it is really important to understand that there are different areas of Family Law, which are dealt with separately. I often have clients approach me who presume that all matters need to be dealt with at the same time; however, for various reasons, that is not usually the case.

Here is a basic overview:

DIVORCE – A divorce requires a court application and does not include court orders for property or children's matters. The divorce application itself is dealt with by another judicial officer (usually a registrar) in proceedings, which run independently of the substantive issues. You cannot apply for a divorce until you have been separated for twelve months, which is one reason the application is dealt with separately (who wants to wait twelve months to resolve urgent parenting and/or property matters?!).

PROPERTY SETTLEMENT – Property settlements set out the division of all of the property when you separate. Many property settlements can be resolved by agreement without court input. A property application with the court can deal with property matters only, or both property and parenting matters combined.

CHILDREN'S MATTERS – Children's matters can often be resolved by agreement without any court input. A parenting application with the court can also seek separate orders for property matters, if applicable.

It is not uncommon to try to negotiate or resolve both property and children's matters at the same time. Likewise, it is not uncommon to have initiated proceedings in relation to one issue only for the other issue to be joined, due to the matter becoming urgent or unable to be resolved.

 *If you are mindful of legal fees, then one of the approaches that you can take is to instruct your solicitor to assist in relation to one area only and act on a self-represented basis for the other area.*

It really depends on the complexity of your matter when it comes to what you would attempt to self-represent in. If you have already engaged a lawyer, then you should have this transparent conversation with them and seek their guidance as to which matter you would be better placed to tackle yourself.

I delve into each of these three areas in more detail later in this book, discussing the ways that the matters can be resolved both outside of court and in a court setting.

Immediate tips post separation

THIS CHAPTER APPLIES TO YOU WHETHER YOU HAVE RECENTLY separated or are contemplating separation. It is worthwhile to read through the practical tips that everyone should consider after separation.

Know your entitlements: Are you de facto?

Did you know that some people do not realise they are in a de facto relationship and have the obligations (or protection) of that relationship status? I have spoken with many clients over the years who did not realise, prior to getting legal advice, that their situation fell under the *Family Law Act*. In some circumstances, you only need to have been living together for two years, or less if you have a child together. Knowing your relationship status is incredibly important. It is one of the first things you should turn your mind to upon separation.

Though the relationship must have existed for at least two years, it is not enough to have simply been together for two years – you need to have been living together on a genuine domestic basis. The Act identifies not only the duration of the relationship but also other considerations, such as: whether there was a sexual relationship, whether you lived together, whether there was financial interdependence, whether property is owned in joint names and whether you would be considered a de facto couple by friends and family. The two-year period can be a continuous period or over stages.

If you have separated and were close to the two-year time period, then it may be in your interest to sever as many of the financial ties with your ex-partner as possible to protect your assets. It may be wise to move out of the family home as soon as possible so that there is no dispute in relation to your separation date (i.e. to ensure that there is evidence that the separation did take place at a certain point and that you were not still in a relationship).

It may be that it is in your interest to be recognised as being in a de facto relationship under the law if the majority of the relationship assets are in your ex-partner's name. If you are not yet separated, you may want to factor that into your separation date or whether you start taking steps to separate your finances or not. Likewise, if you are worried that your partner or ex-partner may have an entitlement to your property, then it may be in your interest to end the relationship sooner rather than later.

Unfortunately, this area of law can be particularly technical and it is one area where I strongly urge you to obtain at least a one-off appointment with a family lawyer who can provide you with advice specific to your particular de facto relationship and perhaps arm you with some tips to protect your financial position.

 *Find out for certain whether you were in a de facto relationship. Even if you need to pay a lawyer for a consultation, it may place you in a better financial position overall and could ultimately save you thousands of dollars.*

Understand your time limits

Knowing the relevant time limits in your matter is critical.

Knowing the time periods you have in which to resolve property matters can save you tens of thousands of dollars.

Beware! There are time limits within which to seek an order from the court for property division. It is amazing how quickly time can fly by! The general rule is that a married couple has twelve months from the date of divorce and a de facto couple has two years from the date of separation to resolve their property matter (this is formalised either by consent agreement or asking for an order of the court, which we will discuss later).

There may be exceptions where you are given leave or permission of the court to ask for property orders if there have been genuine efforts to resolve before the expiration of the time limit, but again each matter is different. Be mindful of these time limits. If it is in your interest for the time limitation to lapse (i.e. significant assets are in your sole name), that is fine, but not if you need to protect your interest in the asset pool.

On the flip side, some married couples take years to get around to even thinking about getting a formal divorce order. If you fail to formalise your property division and there is no divorce order, then it essentially remains open for either party to seek property orders at any stage. I have assisted clients who had been separated for twenty years but never legally divorced *and* never resolved their property settlement. This meant that it was open to them or their ex-partner to seek property division orders based on the property pool at *that* time (not the time of separation). This can be financially devastating for some people.

Please refer to Part Four of the book for more information and tips in relation to property settlements and time limits.

Take copies of documents

Prior to you or your ex-partner leaving the family home, I recommend that you take electronic copies of all financial documents that you have access to. This will include such things as superannuation statements, ATO returns, payslips and bank account statements. Having copies at this point will assist you down the track and help to keep you organised, regardless of whether you are entering into amicable discussions or a high-conflict situation.

Joint bank accounts

Consider speaking with the bank to implement a joint signature requirement on any joint bank accounts, including any redraw facility on a mortgage. It is not uncommon for one person to draw funds from joint bank accounts after separation, and by the time you get to finalising your property settlement, those depleted funds are sometimes either forgotten or difficult to add back into the final division.

In the alternate position, you may yourself want to consider withdrawing funds from a jointly held bank account – particularly if you are leaving the family home and need immediate access to funds to apply towards new living arrangements or for the children. Some clients feel guilty about doing this unilaterally, but remember that you can always return the money or factor it into your property division later.

Familiarise yourself with finances

Were you in charge of the finances during the relationship? Perhaps you have no idea what the assets are or the living expenses were?! It is time to familiarise yourself with the finances as much as possible. In addition to taking copies of key financial documents, also turn your mind to things such as your respective salaries, mortgage repayments, the amount paid on utilities and other bills. Familiarise yourself with insurance details and premiums. Can your accountant provide you with some of the information? It's advisable to make these enquiries with your accountant as soon as possible after separation.

Do you need a caveat?

Do you know if the family home or any of the properties of

the relationship are in sole or joint names? Often, clients who have recently separated are not actually sure how property is held or whose name the title is in. It is fairly straightforward and inexpensive to have a conveyancer or lawyer assist you to do a property search. You can also do your own title searches online (each state has different government bodies to conduct the searches). Searches can be made for properties that you know the address of and you can also search your ex-partner's name (or your own name) to confirm property title listings.

It is really important that you know how the titles are held. If a property is in the sole name of your ex-partner, then they may sell or transfer the property without your knowledge or consent. If this is a genuine concern that you hold, then you should consider lodging a caveat on the title, which precludes your ex-partner from dealing with the property. This will ensure the property is not sold or transferred and protects your interest in that property.

TIPS TO CONSIDER STRAIGHT AWAY:

- *Know your relationship status – were you de facto?*
- *Know your time limits.*
- *Take copies of documents.*
- *Review joint bank accounts.*
- *Familiarise yourself with finances.*
- *Decide if you need a caveat.*

4

Taking back control

THE KEY WORD HERE IS *CONTROL*. WHEN GOING THROUGH A separation and experiencing the losses that you are experiencing, you can feel as though your life is completely out of control. There may be times when you feel *in* control, but other times when you feel as though you have completely lost your way. And, to be perfectly honest, there are definitely things that you simply can't control during this time in your life.

The more in control you are of your situation, however, the better decisions you are likely to make and, in turn, the more likely you are to save money.

Something that I frequently tell my clients is that they do not have control over how their ex-partner deals with the separation. No matter how you style your approach or the tactics you use, the way in which your ex-partner responds or engages is simply out of your control. You can't control how they behave and how they communicate with you. However, I think it is helpful to consider the things that you *can* control when navigating your separation and perhaps the stress of the Family Law system.

The best advice I can give you, from a Family Law perspective, is to control what you can control.

There are a number of practical things that you can do to feel more in control of your separation.

Be organised

One of the most helpful things that you can do is to remain as organised as possible. Please do not be one of those clients who comes into their lawyer's office with a shopping bag full of documents! That's even worse if you are navigating separation or the legal system yourself. You will not know which documents you are looking for or how to find them quickly and easily. Organisation can give you a greater sense of control of your situation.

I suggest you start keeping a notebook purely in relation to your separation. You can start writing relevant notes, which you can refer to later if need be. Take notes when you receive legal advice or when you speak to your financial advisor. Take notes when you speak to any service provider. The types of notes would include, usually in chronological order: the date of the conversation, contact phone numbers, the name of the person that you spoke to, and any main points or advice received. If you are speaking to different counsellors, service providers, lawyers and so on, then keep all of your notes together. Otherwise you will likely get confused or forget information. This is a good idea even if your separation has been amicable so far.

If there is likely to be a property settlement, then start putting together a chronology of events, including the date of purchase of real estate, property values and so on. You should also keep all bank statements, superannuation statements and other financial documents in order by holding them in a hardcopy folder or electronic folders. These documents are what we call discovery material. If you are negotiating a matrimonial or de facto property settlement, then they will likely need to be exchanged at some point, even if your separation is relatively amicable.

If there is a dispute in relation to children and parenting matters, then start keeping notes in a notebook immediately – again, even if things are amicable at this point. This is generally my advice to clients when they first approach me for legal advice and their separation is relatively fresh. Hopefully, your matter is not in court and will not reach that point. However, it may be that there is mediation or litigation in the future and these notes and records can be critical. The notes may be as simple as jotting down the times that you have had the children in your care, or the time that your ex-partner has spent with the children. You may record the dates and times of telephone calls if there is no regular pattern. If the children are struggling with handovers, then you may keep a written record of this. If you have received some legal advice or made contact with a mediation service or service provider, then also write that down in your notebook in chronological order (or in an organised manner that makes sense to you). Keep all of the names of the people that you speak to and their contact details, to ensure that you can easily access the information at a later date if need be.

It can be difficult to remember these specific details further down the track, particularly as you try to deal with the emotional toll and perhaps financial stress of the separation. Your children are presumably the most precious thing in your life. So when it comes to disputes around them, keeping a notebook of all relevant details will ensure you don't forget anything important. It can also help to provide perspective and clarification for any mediation process that may take place.

Obtain new contact details

Are you finding the process stressful? Are you feeling anxious each time you see correspondence or have to communicate with your lawyer or ex-partner? If so, I suggest you seriously turn your mind to setting up a new secure email account for Family Law purposes. This is the email address that you give out for all things in relation to your Family Law matter only. This gives you control so that you can manage when you see correspondence. It ensures that you are not receiving constant reminders of the difficult situation that you are in. If you are up against a fee-generating lawyer who is constantly pushing out correspondence, then this option allows you to reduce your anxiety and receive less-regular distractions. It may also make it easier for you to find correspondence, as it is all in one place.

If you can afford to do so, then you may also consider leasing a PO Box from Australia Post. While most correspondence is sent electronically these days, there may be some hard mail exchanged as well.

Also remember to change the passwords to your email accounts, social media accounts, Apple ID, banking and other log-in details. This is something that you should attend to immediately if you have not done so already.

 *Set up new communication channels for all things for your Family Law file.*

Arm yourself with knowledge

I cannot stress how important it is for you to be realistic and to be informed. This is going to go a long way towards reducing your stress and saving you money.

Do you know what social science says about parenting matters?

Do you have some sort of general knowledge about what is considered in property matters?

There are so many misconceptions in Family Law. Just because your friend has a week-on-week-off shared care arrangement for her children does not mean it is suitable in your circumstances. There has been a misconception around, and presumption of equal shared care since the 2006 amendments to the *Family Law Act*. What the law actually says is that the starting point is equal shared parental *responsibility*. Parental responsibility is very much different from equal time. Parental responsibility centres on issues such as health, education and religion.

Is your ex entitled to half of your superannuation? Again, another common myth. There is also the misconception that the whole property pool should be divided 50/50 in every matter. Each matter differs and your particular and unique circumstances are relevant to how your matter should be resolved.

The fact that you are taking time out to read this book and arm yourself with knowledge is empowering.

You may or may not receive legal advice. Even if you do obtain legal advice or engage a lawyer, you should still ensure that you have some basic information around what your rights are and what the process involves. Even if your separation is amicable and you have reached an agreement, you should still arm yourself with knowledge, formalise the agreement and protect your interests moving forward.

If you have a lawyer, then ask them for links to relevant articles or information that they recommend is relevant to your matter. If you do not have a lawyer, then you may want to read legal blogs or information from legal websites. My law firm, The Family Law Project, produces many helpful videos on social media, runs free webinars and also has resources on YouTube. These videos are presented in a way that is informative and accessible to the layperson. We have purposely created the content in this way to avoid 'legalese'. There are a few law firms like mine that run free webinars and these can be a really helpful resource, even if you have a lawyer. Don't be afraid to sign up for various law firms' newsletters or free webinars. Sure, you're likely to be added to a database, but if you don't get value from the information you are receiving, then ending things is usually as simple as pressing 'unsubscribe'!

 ***Sign up for law firms' newsletters and free webinars.***

There are also many parenting courses, which can be particularly useful if you want to improve your parenting and/or co-parenting skills. You can obtain details from services such as Relationships Australia or the Family Relationships Centre. Both are government funded and often the first port of call for separation advice, counselling referrals, parenting course referrals, anger management course referrals and mediation services.

The Circle of Security International Parenting Course is an excellent parenting course and highly recommended to all parents. It can help to address your children's attachment issues and build emotional resilience, which is particularly important after separation. The course also helps you to understand your children's needs and emotions, and to ensure they feel secure. If your matter is likely to be litigated, then you are putting your best foot forward by completing these courses prior to being ordered to do so by the court.

You may also save money this way, as it will avoid any delays in the proceedings that result from waiting for you to complete a parenting course or anger management course before your matter is considered further. You do not need a lawyer to refer you to these services and you can link in with the courses at any time.

Engage in a low-cost Family Law course.

The Family Law Project offers an online legal education course that you may wish to consider. For more details, visit: www.familylawproject.com.au

Beware of social media

I have already discussed the dangers of relying on well-meaning friends and family members for legal advice. The inaccurate information could ultimately cost you thousands of dollars! Similarly, when arming yourself with knowledge, please avoid relying on internet searches or 'Lawyer Google' too much. I am involved in a few online forums where men and women provide support to each other through their separation and loss. While many of these online forums are well-intentioned and do indeed offer much-needed support, I remain very concerned about some of the information I see in these forums as it is often incorrect.

There are other concerns in relation to social media that could end up costing you more money and causing more stress, so be aware that social media is not necessarily your friend! Time and time again, as lawyers, we see screenshots of the ex-partner's Facebook newsfeed or our client's newsfeed featuring inappropriate comments or incriminating posts. We are not allowed to tell our clients to delete incriminating posts, but we do advise all new clients to cease making them! Reflect on whom you are connected to via social media channels and whether your posts are appropriate. Also ensure you have your settings on 'private' to ensure that you have more control around who is seeing your posts. If you do end up in court, then dealing with and responding to social media criticism can end up costing you more money.

 *Be careful what you post on social media!*

Wear your business hat

Are you able to think of your separation as a business transaction? I know it's easier said than done. But if you can try to remove at least some of the emotion from it, this will help you through the process.

I tell clients to try to put on their 'business hat' when dealing with all things in relation to their separation. As much as possible, remain civil and courteous with both your ex-partner and your lawyer, if you have one. Maintaining civil communication can contribute to the successful resolution of any property or parenting matter. That, in turn, is likely to reduce any feelings of stress and minimise any expenses.

In a pre-mediation session, a social worker advised one of my clients to treat her ex-partner in a businesslike fashion. Be businesslike, be formal, be direct and be polite. In my view, this is not only important in relation to face-to-face communication, but all forms of written communication as well. Keep in mind that, from time to time (if not frequently), you will be met with terse and rude communication. You need to do your best to keep any response polite and businesslike.

 *Put your business hat on!*

If you do communicate directly with your ex-partner, then please do *not* show them copies of any correspondence or written advice that your lawyer has sent you (if you have a lawyer) and do not show them any draft documents which are not intended for them until finalised. It is a positive sign that you would like to keep the lines of communication open with your ex-partner. However, you also need to protect your position (whether financial or in relation to parenting matters).

If you are negotiating with your ex-partner (or their lawyer) directly and do not have a lawyer yourself, then be mindful that anything you write to them via letter, email, text message or social media is not done so on a 'without prejudice' basis, meaning that it may be annexed to a court affidavit if your matter ends up in court. Lawyers often draft correspondence and offers of settlement on a 'without prejudice' basis, meaning that the other party is precluded from revealing the contents of the correspondence and offering it to the court. This allows and encourages a freer exchange of letters of negotiation and proposals for settlements. It can protect your position and is designed to encourage negotiation and help reach an agreement sooner. It encourages proposals to be exchanged that are perhaps more generous and more pragmatic than a formal position would be in the court process.

Batch tasks as necessary

Many of my clients are incredibly stressed and overwhelmed

at various stages through their separation journey. Sometimes they struggle to communicate and to meet deadlines. I have had clients who are notorious for not answering telephone calls or checking messages – no doubt because they find the whole experience too upsetting. Regardless of whether you have a lawyer or not, consider 'batching' tasks and set them aside for times when you feel you are mentally strong enough to complete them.

Another way to describe batching is to *compartmentalise*. This involves separating things into smaller categories to feel more in control and to make things more manageable. Compartmentalising can be particularly useful when you are feeling a strong sense of overwhelm or when your energy is depleted. Some days, you may wake up knowing that there is no way you will have a productive day, and other days you may wake up fired up and ready to go. By batching or compartmentalising, you'll allow yourself to get on with things on your good days when you know you will be in the right mindset.

One client recently said to me, *'No offence, but I hate receiving your emails!'* I know that it is quite rare for a client to want to speak with me and it can act as a trigger for all sorts of emotions. I imagine it's a similar story when speaking to a financial advisor or a mediator. This is another reason I recommend setting up a separate email address, used solely for correspondence in relation to your separation. It may be the same email address that you use to communicate with your ex-partner and is another way that you can batch tasks by only checking that email account from time to time and turning off notifications on your mobile phone.

 *Group all tasks related to your Family Law matter and set aside time in your diary to deal with issues in relation to your separation.*

Understand grief & loss

Separation can be one of the most traumatic experiences you ever go through. It can also be one of the most significant *losses* that you may ever experience. Regardless of whether you were married or in a de facto relationship, you are likely experiencing feelings of loss and grief since your separation. Nobody goes into a relationship to break up! It is irrelevant whether your separation was amicable or high conflict – the sense of loss is likely to be present.

Grief is an emotional response to a loss and everyone will deal with the loss differently. However, having a better understanding of this concept will help you to better resolve your property or parenting matter with your ex-partner. It will help you understand your emotions and why you might be thinking or behaving a certain way. In addition, it is critical to understand that your ex-partner is likely experiencing these different emotions as well. Recognising that is going to be very helpful for you during the negotiation stage.

I wrote the book *Separate Ways: Surviving Post-Separation Grief, the Stress of Divorce or Separation, and the Family Law Process* to really take a deep-dive look into the stages of grief and loss and how they apply in the context of separation. I will only touch on this topic briefly here, but I do recommend that you have a read of *Separate Ways* and other resources around grief and loss in a Family Law context.

The types of loss that you **and** your ex-partner may be experiencing are:

- The loss of your family
- The loss of your spouse/partner
- The loss of a child
- A loss of identity
- A financial loss
- The loss of your family home
- The loss of the 'future family'
- The loss of extended relationships

Almost anyone who has separated has lost the hopes, dreams and expectations they had for the future. Nobody goes into a relationship thinking that it will *not* be successful.

The stages of grief that may apply to you and your ex-partner are:

1. Denial
2. Anger
3. Bargaining
4. Depression
5. Acceptance

Not everybody goes through each stage and it is not chronological or linear. If you are able to research and better understand the stages, then it may help explain the reason you or your ex-partner are behaving or negotiating in a certain way. For example, does your ex-partner have their 'head in the sand' (denial)? Is the communication style aggressive (anger – perhaps masking the pain)? Are there empty promises or threats or last-ditch efforts (bargaining)?

Keep in mind that when someone is in the bargaining stage, they are not likely to be thinking clearly, may be struggling to find meaning, and will do anything possible to repair the relationship. It can be extremely difficult to negotiate during this stage. It is often at this point that I see clients give instructions such as: *'I don't care, he can have the house, I will walk away,'* or *'She can have the children.'* Sometimes we see people being taken advantage of during this time because the agreements they are negotiating are not in their interest.

If you or your ex-partner are experiencing depression, then you are also likely to make poor decisions during this time. This is when we see people making irrational financial decisions, withholding children and showing a disregard for court orders.

Take the time to acknowledge your loss and also recognise that your ex-partner is experiencing their own loss. Researching and understanding the stages of grief in the context of separation is likely to be of huge assistance in your negotiation style and may get you a better result, even saving you thousands of dollars. It will likely also assist you to understand that there may be times when you are tempted to make grief-driven decisions which are not in your interest.

 **Research the stages of grief in the context of separation – my book *Separate Ways: Surviving***

Post-Separation Grief, the Stress of Divorce or Separation, and the Family Law Process is a good place to start.

Understand that nobody is a winner

Unfortunately, it is very rare that a client will feel as though they have had a 'win' in the Family Law space. From time to time, clients will be very pleased with their property settlement negotiations, but it is hard to quantify a 'win' in parenting matters. Due to the stress involved in that process, nobody who ends up in the Family Law Courts is likely to feel as though they have triumphed.

 If you can, try to avoid the 'winning' attitude.

One suggestion that I have for clients who have recently separated is to work out a plan at the outset around what is important to you. This is not so much about what constitutes a 'win', but rather finding things to focus on and to go back and reassess throughout the process. What is important to you? Your plan or wish list may include things such as:

- Ensuring the children live with me the majority of the time.
- Keeping the children in the family home.
- Keeping all of my superannuation.
- Being able to refinance to stay in the family home.
- Being able to refinance to buy my own house.
- Being paid a certain amount so that I am able to start afresh.

- Maintaining an amicable relationship with my ex-partner.
- Focusing on co-parenting the children.

Get preliminary Family Law advice immediately

As a lawyer, it's to be expected that I recommend you obtain independent legal advice as soon as possible.

In the next part of the book, I discuss options such as approaching a free legal service in the first instance, such as your Legal Aid commission or a community legal service. However, if you are able to engage a lawyer, then I recommend that you do – even if only for some preliminary advice and guidance. My strong advice is to **do this as soon as possible.**

The law doesn't require you to have a lawyer at any point (unless you are formalising your property division by a binding financial agreement), but advice from the right kind of lawyer can be invaluable. I strongly recommend you read through the next couple of chapters, even if you have no intention of engaging a lawyer on an ongoing basis.

TIPS – TAKING BACK CONTROL:

- *Be organised – keep a notebook and a hardcopy folder/ electronic files.*
- *Set up separate contact details for Family Law communications.*

- *Arm yourself with knowledge – sign up for law firms' newsletters and free webinars.*
  Look up The Family Law Project's online legal education course: www.familylawproject.com.au
- *Watch what you post on social media and check your security settings.*
- *Be businesslike, be formal, be direct and be polite.*
- *Batch your tasks and deal with them when you're in the right mindset.*
- *Acknowledge your loss and understand the stages of grief in the context of separation.*
- *Make a plan around what is important to you, but don't succumb to the 'winning' mindset.*
- *Obtain independent legal advice as soon as possible.*

PART TWO:
LAWYERS

5

Finding a lawyer

THERE ARE MANY COWBOY LAWYERS OUT THERE WHO WILL happily take you on as a client. And you'll find that many generalist firms 'dabble' in various jurisdictions. It may be that their hourly rate seems appealing and that they seem like a cheaper option compared to a specialist firm. I would offer a word of caution, however. It's best not to consult a lawyer who does not specialise in Family Law.

You should not feel limited if you live in a country town or remote area, as many firms these days will consult via video call and also by telephone. The advantage of a specialist family lawyer is that the jurisdiction is national (with some exceptions in WA), so you do not need to feel limited by a postcode. My firm has clients from all around Australia – these days, the use of technology enables it. The difficulty with a generalist firm, even if they are 'cheap', is that they are likely to be:

- Slower to complete work;
- Not across the legal issues;
- Not well respected in the jurisdiction; and

- Unable to put you in the best possible legal position.

 *Only consult with a specialist family lawyer.*

Junior lawyers have their place

Likewise, take caution if instructing a junior solicitor. I recall my first role as a new graduate and I was extremely 'green'. I also did not have much guidance or support from my employer. I was shown my office, given around sixty files and off I went! Despite being junior, I was charging similar rates to my seniors. I was certainly learning in the role – it was a fantastic learning opportunity for me! But perhaps not the best experience for my clients.

I also recall a few years later when I commenced court work for the first time and was appearing in the Adelaide Registry most days. I was still considered 'green' by my senior solicitors and barristers, who I now realise were smiling assassins! How do I know this? Well, now I'm in their shoes. When I appear in court now, I consider myself to have an advantage over a junior lawyer and I will certainly use their lack of experience to my client's advantage. Nothing scares a junior more than saying, with confidence and a cheeky chuckle, *'Let's just make submissions before the judge and see what s/he says....!'* The reality is that any junior commencing court work will likely prefer to have orders made by negotiation and agreement in the court hallway, rather than make submissions and argue in front of a judge. Will this get you the best possible outcome?

That said, using a paralegal or junior lawyer to complete easier tasks can be an effective way to save on legal fees. I will discuss this later.

 *While engaging a junior may be cheaper, only instruct them if you know that they have a mentor and that the firm is professional in providing the junior with adequate supervision.*

Referrals

Do you know someone who has gone through the process? It may be that they can recommend the lawyer they engaged. They will know firsthand how they felt about the particular lawyer based on their experience with them. They may also know firsthand which lawyers to avoid! My firm often has new clients approach us upon recommendations from a current or previous client of our firm. My favourite recommendation was made by the opponent in one of my matters, who was self-represented. I had made things a little difficult for the poor guy. From a lawyer's perspective, this was the highest of compliments because while I did a good job for my client, he could also recognise that I had performed well.

 *Remember not to ask your friend for legal advice, but do ask them for a referral/recommendation for a lawyer.*

The different sorts of lawyers

There are also different types of law firms and various types of lawyers to take into consideration.

If you and your ex-partner have had an amicable split, then you are fortunate to have some excellent options for alternative dispute resolution and peaceful settlement options.

If your separation has not been amicable, then you really need to consider what you want from a lawyer. Do you want a lawyer who is aggressive (the so-called 'shark')? Do you want someone who will support you and shows empathy? Someone who is results driven?

 Ask yourself: Do you *really* want the shark lawyer?!

I often change my style to suit my client. My natural style is to keep the communication between the parties amicable and, either way, reach an agreement by consent and out of court. I can up the ante and draft aggressive letters if need be; often, this is guided by my client. It is very important that you consider what style of lawyer has the best approach to get outcomes with your ex-partner.

Please do not confuse a 'good lawyer' with an 'overly litigious lawyer'. My view is that as many matters as possible should be resolved without litigation. If you are working with a litigious lawyer, then you are more likely to end up in court, which may end up costing you.

TIPS – FINDING A LAWYER:

- *Only consult with a lawyer who specialises in Family Law.*
- *Only deal with a junior lawyer if you know they have adequate supervision.*
- *Ask friends for referrals/recommendations.*
- *Decide what sort of lawyer you want.*

6

Free legal advice & representation

MANY FIRMS OFFER A FIRST FREE MEETING TO POTENTIAL NEW clients. One of the reasons for this is for both the firm and the client to make an assessment as to whether they are the 'right fit'. It is very important when you instruct a solicitor that you are not only confident in their legal abilities, but also comfortable with them. It is for this reason that I generally suggest to new potential clients that they consult with another one or two solicitors by way of comparison.

Engaging a lawyer is a big decision and can be costly. It is important that you make this choice on an informed basis. It is not uncommon for clients to cry during or at the end of their free meeting with us. It is often a sign of relief – they know they will be guided through the process. Do you feel that sense of relief when meeting with your potential lawyer? They do not need to be likeable, but you may be stuck with this person/firm for some time, so ensure they are the right fit. How are their people skills? Likewise, how has your experience been with the firm from start to finish? How were the reception staff or paralegals whom you spoke with prior to the meeting? How were you greeted? How did you feel at the office? Do you think you will be supported through the process?

It is important to consider what is right for *you*. It may not be important to you that the lawyer is likeable. You may feel confident based on their knowledge that you are in good hands. I know that I have personally paid a lawyer for a non-Family-Law-related matter because they were an expert in their area of law. I was not particularly drawn to the lawyer's personality, but the matter was urgent and I was very outcome driven at the time. I had confidence in his ability to guide me through that process.

It is similar to when we brief barristers. My firm does a lot of in-house court work, but from time to time we do brief external barristers. We generally recommend a barrister (a Family Law specialist, naturally!) based on the particular client and who we think will be a suitable match for them. It is not uncommon for me to advise clients that our selection is based on the barrister's specific legal and advocacy knowledge as opposed to their people skills. This acts as a heads-up that the barrister is very valuable and there for a purpose, but don't expect general chit chat about your weekend!

Keep in mind that most first free interviews will only be around thirty minutes. There is limited time to go into your matter in detail. It will, however, give you a good feel for the lawyer and their Family Law knowledge. Be prepared and use the opportunity to get as much procedural information as possible relevant to your particular circumstances.

 *Take advantage of a first free meeting with more than one law firm, even if you do not think that you will engage a lawyer. It will help you to obtain procedural and general legal information relevant to your matter.*

You'll find further tips in the next chapter in relation to how to prepare for your first meeting with a lawyer.

Pro bono representation

My law firm is sometimes approached by potential clients enquiring whether we conduct pro bono work. Pro bono work is very limited in Family Law matters and you are unlikely to find many private lawyers conducting it. Unfortunately, as a small business assisting many legal aid clients and reduced-fixed-fee clients, we are unable to offer pro bono services.

You will find that most 'big boy firms' do not do any legal aid work and certainly do not conduct pro bono work in this jurisdiction. I have previously worked for private firms and had the opportunity to do pro bono work in other areas, such as immigration. Despite Australian firms dedicating hundreds of thousands of hours each year to pro bono matters, I suspect you will have trouble finding a firm to assist in this respect in your Family Law matter.

Legal aid assistance

Many people think that they need to qualify for legal aid to receive *assistance* from a Legal Aid office. The reality is that receiving a grant of legal aid is both means and merit based (i.e. you need to be in receipt of a Centrelink benefit/very low income and your matter needs to have merit). I have worked for Legal Aid offices in both South Australia and New South Wales and can say that both states (along with all states in Australia) offer an excellent advice service which is *not* means or merit based.

An advice service is just that. It will assist to point you in the right direction and the advisor will likely give you some good procedural information. You cannot expect a lengthy session or ongoing representation unless you qualify for a grant of legal aid for representation, but it can be a good starting point. Most offices also offer a referral service to law firms who may be able to assist you.

You may not qualify for a grant of legal aid for ongoing representation. However, you are likely to be able to use the Legal Aid free advice service (which is not means tested). This can be a good first port of call. Arm yourself with as much knowledge as possible, even if you do not intend to engage a solicitor.

Legal aid funding

Will you qualify for legal aid representation? When applying for legal aid, you may be assigned an in-house or external lawyer from a private law firm who accepts grants of legal aid funding. I suggest that you meet with private lawyers who accept legal aid assignments before applying for legal aid. If they are happy to act for you, then you can nominate the law firm on your application form so that Legal Aid assigns your matter to that particular lawyer. Law firms who conduct legal aid work are not necessarily any good. Some will cut corners! Others are not specialists in Family Law. If you do not nominate your preferred lawyer, then it is a bit like a lucky dip and you don't know who will be assigned as your lawyer.

National legal aid funding is at a crisis and my experience is that fewer matters are being funded. My law firm sees firsthand the restrictions in funding for the clients we assist under a grant of legal aid.

Meet with a private lawyer who undertakes legal aid work. If you would like them to represent you, then ensure you request any legal aid funding is assigned to their office. There are also some excellent lawyers who work for Legal Aid and you can request them by name if you have met with them or they have been recommended to you. You are able to nominate your lawyer and there will be no additional cost to you if you nominate a lawyer from a private law firm.

If your matter is in relation to parenting, then you might receive legal aid funding for lawyer-assisted mediation or for court proceedings. Again, you may be allocated an in-house lawyer or a private lawyer who accepts legal aid assignments.

If your matter is in relation to property issues, then you are unlikely to qualify for legal aid unless you are essentially dividing superannuation or debt. In the past, we have received limited funding to assist a vulnerable person to negotiate property settlements, to apply to court for urgent spousal maintenance or an injunction in relation to sale of property, and also to divide superannuation. If there is equity in your property, then Legal Aid is likely to take the view that you would be in a position to pay legal fees from that equity.

Having said that, some state Legal Aid offices have introduced funding for lawyer-assisted mediations to resolve small asset pools.

If you have a very small asset pool or the only asset is superannuation, then it is worthwhile applying for legal aid funding to see if you qualify for assistance with your property settlement.

Regardless of whether your matter is in relation to parenting or property matters, if you own property, then you can expect to have to sign a 'consent to statutory charge'. This is essentially permission for a charge to be registered on your certificate of title for you to repay your legal fees. I am aware of some clients being reluctant to sign a consent to statutory charge; however, generally speaking, the amount that you would have to repay as a legal aid client would be approximately a third of the fees compared to paying on a private basis. It is also worthwhile noting that the fees are not repaid until you sell or transfer the property at a later date.

Please do not make the mistake of presuming that you will not qualify for legal aid. If in doubt, then apply! I am horrified at the number of cases I have taken over for clients who were paying lawyers on a private basis when they qualified for legal aid. It is generally the case that a family member is funding their legal fees until they run out of money, and then the client is advised that they would actually qualify for legal aid. I have seen this happen with numerous clients whose family members have paid tens of thousands of dollars in legal fees on their behalf.

It is not uncommon for my firm to 'inherit' these files from other law firms after all of the extended family's money has been exhausted. It is also not uncommon for these clients not to realise that they might have actually qualified for legal aid all along. This is a topic that really fires me up! As lawyers, we have a duty and obligation to advise clients that they may qualify for legal aid. My blood also boils to learn that many of these clients who have spent tens of thousands of dollars can no longer be represented by their law firm because the firm does not accept grants of legal aid funding.

 *Don't let your unsuspecting family members pay all of your legal fees if you actually qualify for a grant of legal aid!*

Most states also provide some limited legal aid funding as a one-off to assist a client in the first instance. If you apply for legal aid, then the Legal Aid office might want the lawyer to provide them with further information about your matter and make some recommendations as to whether you should have more extensive funding for lawyer-assisted mediation or for court. Even if you do not qualify for any further funding, this limited funding is a good opportunity for you to meet with a lawyer and obtain that more detailed and specific legal advice. It can really offer a bit of peace of mind in terms of the options available to you and can be a great starting point.

 *Not sure you will qualify for legal aid? Give it a shot or at least make further enquiries.*

Community legal centres

There are many excellent community legal centres (CLCs) in Australia that are funded independently of Legal Aid commissions. These CLCs are also having funding issues and last year they turned away hundreds of thousands of clients. Often, a CLC will be limited to providing advice only (as opposed to representation). However, some CLCs will provide ongoing advice and representation to clients who meet their means and merit guidelines. It is worth checking if there is a CLC near you that can assist, and at least take advantage of their free advice service. You will find, however, that the advice service is similar to a Legal Aid advice service in that the advice is generally quite limited and procedural. It can be a good starting point, though.

CLCs can also be a good resource as they have strong partnerships with non-legal services, such as domestic violence services and health services. They are a good referral source for other Family Law service providers.

 *Make an advice appointment with your local community legal centre. You may qualify for ongoing assistance from them.*

Family Violence & Cross-Examination Scheme

In 2019, the Australian Government introduced additional free legal funding under the Family Violence and Cross-Examination Scheme. Family lawyers know this as 'section 102NA funding'.

The introduced funding can act as a loophole for some people to qualify for free legal representation in court matters where there are allegations of family violence. The funding is not means or merit tested.

The funding was introduced to protect victims of family violence from being cross-examined at trial by perpetrators of violence. Extensive studies have established that the cross-examination of a victim by anyone, let alone the alleged perpetrator, can be re-traumatising. Where one or both parties are self-represented and the parenting or property matter is listed for trial and there has been a conviction or charge of violence or any injunctions, then the court must make an 's102NA Declaration'. That then entitles the parties to funding under the scheme. The funding is administered by the state Legal Aid offices and is not means or merit tested. The impact of the declaration is that the self-represented party (or parties) is not able to cross-examine the other party. Funding will be provided for legal preparation and representation at the trial.

The declaration is also made if the alleged victim is self-represented, as the legislation does not allow the alleged victim to personally cross-examine the alleged perpetrator.

Have there been allegations of family violence in your court matter? If either of you are self-represented or would consider going self-represented, the court could make an order listing your matter for trial so as to 'trigger' the s102NA Declaration.

As one judge described it to me over coffee, *'It is effectively free legal aid which is not means or merit tested.'*

The sooner the declaration is made during the proceedings, the sooner you may qualify for free legal representation.

It does not matter whether you are the alleged perpetrator or the alleged victim. The declaration and free legal representation will apply to both property and parenting matters and it does not matter how high your salary is or what your means are. It means that many people who would not usually qualify for free legal representation may do so under what some see as a loophole.

We once had a client paying our law firm on a private basis because they earned in excess of $200,000 per annum and did not qualify for legal aid. That same client then stopped instructing us for a period and conducted the proceedings on a self-represented basis. The court subsequently made the s102NA Declaration because of allegations of family violence. The client subsequently received the free government funding and re-instructed my firm to act for him under the legal aid funding.

TIPS – OBTAINING FREE LEGAL ADVICE & REPRESENTATION:

- *Take advantage of a first free meeting with more than one law firm.*
- *Take advantage of the Legal Aid free advice service (which is not means tested).*
- *Meet with a private lawyer who undertakes legal aid work or receive recommendations for Legal Aid lawyers so you can nominate your own lawyer in your application.*
- *If you have a very small asset pool or the only asset is superannuation, then it is worthwhile applying for legal aid funding.*
- *Don't let unsuspecting family members pay your legal fees when you actually qualify for legal aid.*
- *Not sure if you qualify for aid? Give it a shot!*
- *Make an advice appointment with your local community legal centre.*
- *If there are allegations of family violence in your court matter, be aware of the loophole for accessing free legal aid through the s102NA Declaration.*

Your first meeting with a lawyer

HAVE YOU HEARD OF THE 'SOPRANOS RULE'? IN *THE SOPRANOS*, Tony goes to every good divorce lawyer in town so that his wife, Carmela, is not allowed to instruct them because they are already 'conflicted'. If you speak with a lawyer prior to your ex-partner doing so, then they will not be able to instruct or get advice from that lawyer due to a conflict of interest. Lawyers have an obligation to keep information confidential.

There were similar reports that Heidi Klum met with many of the best divorce lawyers in Los Angeles following her well-reported separation from Seal. It might be that she was interviewing them to choose the right lawyer for her; however, the result was that enough information was revealed during those initial meetings to block Seal from then instructing and using those lawyers.

I am not suggesting that you use the 'Sopranos Rule' and do what Tony did. I am simply bringing it to your attention to try to avoid the same thing happening to you. Choose the lawyers you want to consider sooner rather than later, and meet with them while you can.

Manage your expectations

Do not have unrealistic expectations around your first meeting with a lawyer, particularly if it is a short meeting. An analogy might be when you make an appointment with your general practitioner. If you have an underlying illness, you wouldn't expect the doctor to provide a diagnosis during that first meeting without having run some tests and done a thorough medical examination.

It is incredibly common for me to chat to a new client for twenty to thirty minutes, and towards the end of the conversation be asked what I think the percentage of division of property should be. It would be negligent for me to answer with certainty. I wish it were that simple, I really do! Be wary of any lawyer who tells you with confidence at the end of a short first meeting that you are entitled to a certain percentage of the asset pool. Likewise, it is difficult, if not impossible, after the short meeting to be able to advise a client with certainty as to what living arrangements for the children would be ordered if the matter were before the court. Having said that, it is generally easier for family lawyers to make a more efficient analysis of a parenting custody matter.

You should expect the lawyer to be able to understand what your needs are and to provide procedural information as to the various legal options available in your type of matter. You should walk away from the meeting or end the telephone/video conference feeling more informed and better assured of the process and options available to you.

 *Ensure that you check the charge of the first free meeting in the event that you exceed the advertised free twenty or thirty-minute allowance.*

The more prepared you can be during your first meeting, the more value you will take from it and the less time you will spend summarising key matters. Many law firms will ask you a number of questions when you first book your appointment. Do not be frustrated by this process but recognise that the more time you spend providing this information online or via administrative staff, the better the lawyer can spend their time with you. My firm will always spend some time speaking to the client when they book the appointment to ask questions about key dates and, time permitting, some basic details in relation to their matter to get a brief overview. This means that the lawyer is not going in blind and has a rough idea of what your needs are in advance.

Chronology document

I suggest that you prepare a chronology to take with you to the appointment. Ensure that it is also in electronic format so that it can be emailed to the firm if you ultimately instruct them. Consider your chronology a 'go to' cheat sheet for your lawyer. It should provide a brief overview of all key dates, such as: commencement of relationship, commencement of living together, marriage (if applicable), date of separation, date of divorce (if applicable), dates of acquisition of key assets (and cost of same), birth dates of children, any key inheritances and so on. It should not be overly detailed for that first meeting.

In addition to the chronology, I recommend that you prepare a summary of assets and liabilities for property settlement matters. The summary should itemise each major asset, offer an estimated value and confirm whether it is held in sole or joint names. It should also include whether the asset has been formally valued and whether the value has been agreed upon by the other party.

My view is that having the chronology and list of assets is much more valuable during that first meeting than taking the actual valuations/appraisals themselves. Certainly, a lawyer is not going to be wanting to look at documents such as bank statements, superannuation statements or valuations in detail during that short initial meeting.

 *Be prepared. Have a list of assets and liabilities (for property matters) and a short chronology (for both parenting and property matters).*

Ditch the Woolworths bag

You may recall that earlier in this book I spoke about the importance of being organised and putting on your 'business hat'. It may seem obvious, but it is very important to keep everything together in one folder, where it is easy for you to access. I suggest creating an electronic folder and having all relevant documents scanned and saved in sub folders also. This keeps things nice and organised, removes some stress (you're already under enough stress) and makes it quick and easy to share with your lawyer. Don't waste five minutes (or worse still, seven minutes for those lawyers working in six-minute intervals!) searching for your superannuation statement.

Having worked in this jurisdiction for close to twenty years, I can say that it is still not uncommon for the odd client to present at the first or subsequent meeting with paperwork stashed in a Woolworths bag. Argh!

TIPS – YOUR FIRST MEETING WITH A LAWYER:

- *Be prepared. Have a list of assets and liabilities (for property matters) and a short chronology (for both parenting and property matters).*
- *Ensure that you check the charge of the first free meeting in the event that you exceed the advertised free period.*
- *Ditch the Woolies bag. Keep everything well organised in a physical folder and also an electronic folder.*

8

Communications with a lawyer

As a family lawyer, I often feel like a social worker. But have you considered how much you would pay a counsellor or social worker per hour? I suspect it would be less than a lawyer's hourly rate. My point is that you should go into every meeting with a lawyer valuing *your* time and, therefore, not spending ten minutes delving into detail about your ex-partner having an affair with the postman. It is not a good use of your time, whether you are in a free meeting with a lawyer or paying for their service!

I find it important to show empathy to my clients, and I am certainly not going to stop them from giving me information if they are upset or feel it is important for them to tell me. But if cost is a concern, it's important to keep on track. I suspect many lawyers will allow you to ramble as long as you want if they are being paid per six-minute interval! Context is important. If you want a referral for mental health support, then you should ask; however, try to keep the mental health discussions to a minimum with your lawyer if you are wanting to best utilise your time. Be aware there are many free mental health support services available, including free consultations with a psychologist pursuant to a mental health care plan.

During the times that you interact with your lawyer, I suggest that you think of the communication as a business transaction. It's more easily said than done, but do your best to remove some of the emotion from your dealings and instructions.

 *Do not treat your lawyer like a social worker.*

Write down your questions and take notes

What do you want to achieve when you meet with a lawyer – whether it is a free meeting or ongoing meetings with a lawyer who is representing you? Be clear about this. What are your burning questions? What are the things that are unclear to you at the moment that you would like explained (preferably without the legal jargon!). The next tip is really simple, but very important. Write down your questions. You may find that you are nervous or emotional during the meeting. You may be learning new terminology and concepts from the lawyer and be easily distracted or forget your key questions. If you have a list, by the conclusion of the meeting, you can ensure all your questions have been answered.

 *Write down your key questions prior to every meeting with a lawyer or legal advisor.*

It is also important to jot down notes on anything that you need to action or any important advice given to you during the meeting itself. Information is too easily forgotten in these circumstances and good note taking can save some serious cash. You don't want to be repeating the same questions if you do not need to.

 *Buy a book in which to take notes and jot down points when speaking with legal advisors. Keep all of the information together.*

Having a support person

Another issue to consider is whether you take a friend or family member with you when you meet with a lawyer. If you do this, remember that, ultimately, it is *you* providing instructions. Do not allow the well-meaning friend or family member to speak on your behalf. Speak with them beforehand to confirm that their role is to provide support and possibly take notes if you do not feel as though you can take your own.

 *If you are too emotional or confused to jot down notes, then have your support person do this for you.*

Remember, if you already have your list of important points/questions, then you are not likely to miss anything, so there really is no need for your support person to speak or barrack on your behalf.

In my experience, a well-meaning supporter can sometimes act as a hindrance, so be mindful of this. An example is where your support person is not privy to the numerous conversations that you have already had with your lawyer or the information and documents you have already provided. There is a risk that the support person will want to retell your story and ensure that the lawyer is aware of everything. They may also ask questions that you already know the answer to. I see this time and time again, particularly when a support person comes along towards the end of a matter (for example, at trial stage at court). There have been times when I have had to ask the support person to leave my meeting room or to leave me alone with the client at court because they are distracting us from what we should be focusing on. The problem with this kind of well-meaning support person is that they can eat into your valuable time with your lawyer.

That said, there is a lot to be said for having a support person whose role it is to take notes on your behalf and ensure that your pre-prepared questions are answered. They can also be fantastic as someone to debrief with after your meetings or critical events. They just need to be clear about their role.

TIPS – COMMUNICATIONS WITH YOUR LAWYER:

- *Value your time when meeting with your lawyer – do not treat them like a social worker. Instead, put your business hat on.*
- *Write down key questions prior to every meeting.*
- *Jot down notes about anything that you need to action or any important advice given to you.*
- *Consider whether you will benefit from having a support person present at meetings.*

How to choose a lawyer (if you decide to get one)

ONCE YOU HAVE SPOKEN WITH A FEW LAWYERS AND/OR received some guidance from Legal Aid or a community legal centre, then you will need to make a decision whether to engage a lawyer or whether to brave it alone.

At the outset, and straight up, I want to give you the following tip:

 *The most expensive lawyer is not always the best!*

But:

 *Looking for the cheapest lawyer is not necessarily going to get you the best outcome either!*

Transparency

My view is that the key to making a decision about which lawyer to choose is transparency. You want to have a good indication of what your legal fees are going to be. We often have potential clients call our office asking what our hourly rate is. While it is good that clients are making enquiries about fees, I believe that this question can be somewhat moot. If I am asked this, then my response is usually that you need to be careful when asking that question. Do not let that question alone determine whom you instruct. The point is, if my hourly rate were $400 and another firm's were $300, that in itself does not mean that your fees would be less at the other firm.

Lawyers are often subjected to unrealistic billing expectations by their employer or they may be on generous bonus schemes. Someone charging $300/hour can easily generate significantly more in legal fees if they are undertaking more work than is required in your matter. Lawyers know the tricks of the trade when it comes to the 'billable hour' and working in six-minute intervals. Meanwhile, one law firm may have a higher hourly rate, but they may be outcome driven and more focused on achieving a quick result for you.

I am aware that many private practitioners are subjected to weekly meetings in relation to their billable targets and KPIs. Why haven't they reached their targets? How can more fees be generated? What is the additional work that can be done on a file? These lawyers are essentially looking to create work on your case! I know of lawyers who have to justify how they spend their day and the reason that they have not met billing targets. One lawyer recently told me that she started recording everything that she was doing during the day, even toilet breaks, to justify to her employer where her time was being spent. Talk about billing pressure!

When it comes to unnecessary work, here are some initial examples that come to mind without having to think too hard:

- Lawyers who draft and send ungodly long letters with repetitive and perhaps unnecessary information;

- Lawyers who drag out the discovery (document exchange) process in property settlement matters by requesting or providing more documentation than is perhaps necessary;

- Lawyers who spend an unreasonable amount of time and (your) money briefing a barrister when it is not completely necessary;

- Solicitors who appear as an 'instructing solicitor' with a barrister at a directions hearing, which does not require both a barrister and a solicitor;

- Lawyers who draft unnecessarily long documents (including consent minutes of order or court documents such as affidavits) to generate fees.

I even know of a law firm who charges their client when the receptionist buzzes the solicitor down the hall to advise them that their client has arrived for a pre-arranged appointment. Outrageous and surely questionable! I hope that these examples help to illustrate that a certain hourly rate is not necessarily indicative that a law firm will provide you with fair and reasonable fees.

While there is nothing wrong with asking a firm what their hourly rate is, be mindful that an hourly rate in itself is not necessarily indicative of fair and reasonable fees. If a lawyer knows how to 'milk your file' or, as an employee, is under immense billing pressure, with KPIs / expected billing hours, then it doesn't matter if their hourly rate is lower – they will find ways to generate fees on your file.

Have you read your cost agreement in detail? They are generally very long. Did you know that most lawyers charge for printing each page, sending each page of a fax and so on? Some lawyers will also send a letter by post and then by email rather than just annexing the letter to the email – you will be charged in duplicate.

TIPS – CHOOSING A LAWYER:

- *The most expensive lawyer isn't always the best.*
- *The cheapest lawyer likely won't be the best either!*
- *Don't judge a lawyer solely on their hourly rate.*

10

Paying your lawyer

ONE WAY TO CREATE CERTAINTY AROUND YOUR LEGAL FEES IS to engage a law firm who offers fixed fees. The benefit of a fixed-fee service is that it provides you with complete transparency. You will not be in a position where you feel as though you are watching the clock for every six-minute interval to pass. You are not dreading every interim invoice, with no idea how much work has been done. You do not avoid the telephone call from your lawyer, knowing that you will pay for each minute of the conversation.

I will take the opportunity to sidestep here and, in defence of lawyers, mention that the work we do is often very complex and is likely more involved than you may realise. Lawyers can spend hours reading through discovery documents. They have the legal experience to know what information to ask for when taking instructions from you to extract critical information, which may, in fact, end up saving you thousands of dollars.

Regardless, the beauty of fixed fees is that you are aware up front what your fees will be. No nasty bill shock.

There are some matters where it is difficult to offer fixed fees. For example, where there is absolute uncertainty as to the amount of work involved or which direction your matter will take. Those particularly tricky matters can make it difficult for a law firm to offer fixed fees.

But ask yourself: If your lawyer is not acting for you under a fixed-fee agreement, where is their incentive to run your matter in an efficient way and in the shortest possible time?

 *Make enquiries with firms as to whether they offer fixed fees. If not, why not?*

If your law firm does not offer fixed fees but you still want to engage them, then continue reading – there are more tips coming on how to save money when instructing such firms.

Scale of Costs

If you do not engage a lawyer on a fixed-fee basis, then ensure that you understand how the time-billed basis for billing works. Know the hourly rates of your lawyer and familiarise yourself with the Scale of Costs (Scale), which each state has in place to regulate legal fees. Is your lawyer charging in line with the Scale? If not, why not? If they are charging over and above the Scale, then you are allowed to ask the law firm about that.

 *If you are confused by the pile of paperwork, then the simple question to ask the law firm is whether they charge in accordance with the Scale.*

Cost agreements

A cost agreement is a written agreement between you and the law firm that sets out the cost arrangements for your matter. The agreement is usually full of legalese.

All law firms are required to provide you with a cost agreement for your consideration prior to commencing work. These are governed by the relevant Law Society, which requires the agreement to have provision that you should obtain legal advice in relation to the cost agreement. The reality is, in my almost twenty years' legal experience, that I have only *once* been instructed by a client to purely review the cost agreement of another law firm. I provided written advice in relation to that cost agreement. Many of the questions that my client had could have been directed to the law firm that she ultimately instructed in her matter.

I am a realist and know that it is unlikely that you are going to fork out hundreds of dollars with another lawyer to obtain legal advice in relation to a cost agreement with your chosen law firm. You should, however, read the agreement extremely carefully. Do you understand your rights and obligations? Can you obtain some free advice from a Legal Aid office or community legal centre in relation to the cost agreement? At the very least, you should put any specific questions in relation to the agreement to the law firm before you engage their services. If they are not willing to take the time to explain the cost agreement, then that might be a good indication that they are not the right law firm for you to instruct.

 *Read your cost agreement carefully. If there's anything you don't understand, ask the question of the law firm and/or seek advice elsewhere.*

Deferred fees

Are you asset rich but cash poor? Do you feel as though you may be entitled to a payment at the conclusion of your property settlement, but at this point in time there is no way that you could meet payment of potential legal fees? Perhaps you were not the main breadwinner in the relationship and now that you have separated, you are surviving on either a Centrelink benefit or a single low income. You should not let this preclude you from reaching out for assistance. Some law firms will offer clients a deferred-fee cost agreement, meaning that you do not need to pay your legal fees up front. Rather, your legal fees will be taken from your anticipated cash payout in the settlement. It may be that the family home is likely to be sold and you are to receive funds from the proceeds of sale. Again, instead of requiring fees up front, your lawyer may be able to defer their fees so that they can be deducted from those proceeds.

The exception to deferred fees, at least at my firm, is that we do not defer the costs of disbursements (out-of-pocket expenses). These costs, such as valuations, reports, filing fees and so on, generally have to be paid up front by the client. Many of these costs are nominal, but you should ask your lawyer to spell them out to you based on your particular circumstances so that you can start putting money aside to meet those costs when they arise.

Asset rich but cash poor? Ensure you make enquiries with a lawyer who will offer a deferred-fee cost agreement. This will often save you money, as you won't have to pay fees on your credit card or take out a loan to fund your fees.

How many lawyers does it take?!

Prior to instructing a law firm, ascertain how many lawyers will be working on your matter. Which lawyers will you be dealing with? If you are not working pursuant to fixed fees, then you need to realise that lawyers of different experience charge different amounts. Will a junior lawyer *and* a senior lawyer be working on your matter? Is it necessary to have two or more lawyers assisting you? Can you save costs by having a junior lawyer conduct the majority of the work? Paralegals are also able to do some of the lower-level tasks.

Avoid duplicating your legal fees by paying for more than one lawyer to perform similar work on your matter. Instruct the firm to have a junior or paralegal complete lower-level tasks.

Trust accounts

In addition to signing a cost agreement prior to the firm commencing work for you, there will likely be an expectation that you will make payment into the law firm's trust account. If the service is for fixed fees, then it will be that specified amount.

If it is not a fixed-fee service, then it will be another amount as nominated by the firm. It is usual practice for law firms to request monies up front.

 **Can't afford the entire amount to be paid into trust? Will the firm offer a payment plan? Spacing out payments can make it more achievable for you. A payment plan is unlikely to be offered to you unless you ask.**

The Law Societies have very strict regulations in relation to trust accounts and law firms are audited annually. Law firms *are* allowed to withdraw any monies without your knowledge or consent. But law firms are *not* allowed to move or invest those monies into an interest-bearing account or earn any interest on those monies.

You are entitled to ask for the balance of your monies held in the trust account at any time. You should also be notified prior to any transfer out of the trust account. If you want to dispute an invoice that has been issued to you, then get onto that quickly. You only have a number of days to notify the law firm prior to them transferring your monies from their trust account to their business account. Ultimately, if there is transparency, and particularly if there are fixed fees, this should not be an issue.

TIPS – PAYING YOUR LAWYER:

- *Engage a firm that offers fixed fees if you can (if not, why not?).*

- *If you are being charged on a billed-time basis, familiarise yourself with the Scale of Costs and check that your lawyer adheres to the Scale.*
- *Read your cost agreement carefully and ask questions.*
- *Asset rich but cash poor? Seek a lawyer who offers a deferred-fee cost agreement.*
- *Understand how many lawyers will be working on your matter and what they each cost. Request that lower-level work is completed by a junior or paralegal.*
- *Unable to pay in full upfront? Enquire whether a payment plan is possible.*

Unbundled legal services

IF YOU HAVE READ THROUGH THE PREVIOUS CHAPTER AND don't think that obtaining a lawyer to represent you throughout the entire process is achievable, then I urge you to get some specific legal advice relevant to your personal circumstances. This is where 'unbundled' legal services come in handy. This enables the provision of legal assistance at various stages throughout your matter.

How might this look? Here are some examples.

- You pay a lawyer for some specific advice and guidance in your matter. For example, you pay a certain amount of money which covers a meeting of up to one hour (or longer), perusal of some documentation and either verbal or written initial advice. This is a good way to receive advice that is *specific* to your situation and it will certainly provide you with better guidance than a first free meeting. Ask for these fees to be fixed.

- You instruct a lawyer to do the above and/or write a letter for you. A lawyer might, for example, take some more detailed instructions and then write to your ex-partner in relation to a concern about a parenting matter. This could involve writing to commence the negotiation process and ascertain whether they are likely to engage in the process. This is a 'test the water' type approach, which can be very helpful in determining which step you take next.

- You have received an offer from your ex-partner in relation to property and/or parenting matters, and you request some further advice in relation to that offer. Ask for those fees to be fixed.

- You have reached an agreement and you want to pay a lawyer to formalise the agreement to ensure that it is legally binding. For property matters, that agreement would be formalised by consent minutes of order or a binding financial agreement. Parenting matters are formalised by way of consent minutes of order or a parenting plan. You should be certain that an agreement has been reached prior to engaging a lawyer to draft the agreement. You do not want to spend money on legal fees for documents to be drafted only to have the other party refuse to sign them. I am often instructed to draft agreements as opposed to providing a full representation service. Be aware that once the documents are drafted, if you seek advice, you may be advised against signing the document.

- You instruct a lawyer to draft certain documents for you. For example, they draft documents to initiate or respond to proceedings in court, while not representing you or attending court. You may instruct a lawyer to read through some of the court documents and to draft an affidavit for you.

- You are not able to pay for a lawyer and barrister to represent you at trial (particularly with prohibitive barrister fees); however, you instruct a lawyer to draft your trial documents so that you are in a much better and more confident position when self-representing through the trial process.

As you can see through the examples above, unbundled legal services enable you to manage your own Family Law matter and target professional legal support at various times. This enables you to have better control of your legal budget and strategically use the services when required.

If you've decided against engaging a lawyer to represent you, don't forget you have the option to access unbundled legal services at any point in the process.

Getting the most out of your lawyer

IF YOU ARE NOT INSTRUCTING YOUR LAWYER ON A FIXED-FEE basis, then go back and read Chapter 10! In all seriousness, if you cannot for some reason fix your fees, then be aware that every contact you have with your law firm will cost you money. Much as you might like to, you can't dispute every item on your bill. I've worked with firms before where the client has disputed costs such as a telephone call because *they* called our office as opposed to the lawyer dialling their number! If you're unsure, your cost agreement will clearly set out everything that you will be charged for and you can confidently presume it will be all points of contact.

Effective communication

One of the most cost-effective ways to communicate with your lawyer is by email. It is more controlled, more organised and you are likely to get to the point more clearly as opposed to during a telephone call or face-to-face meeting, where it is easier to get off track. Check your cost agreement and compare the cost of having your lawyer peruse email correspondence to the cost of telephone calls or face-to-face attendance.

 *Using email to communicate with your law firm can be one of the most cost-effective ways to save in legal fees.*

Pick your battles

If you are not on a fixed-fee cost agreement, then every point of contact with your lawyer will cost you money. There will be a number of issues raised by your ex-partner when negotiating your parenting matter or property settlement, but turn your mind to the cost of disputing each issue. How important is the particular issue to you? How much will it cost for your lawyer to take instructions and write to the other party?

I have recently been assisting a client in relation to her matrimonial property settlement. We were initially negotiating an agreement without using the court system but, unfortunately, her ex-partner initiated court proceedings so her hand was forced. The parties went along to a court-ordered conciliation conference, which is a lawyer-assisted mediation facilitated by a registrar of the court. The parties were able to reach an agreement on the entire property pool, aside from their bird cages and who was going to keep them. I advised my client to try to resolve this matter by negotiation because the reality was that if that remained unresolved, it would not only mean that the rest of the property agreement became unstuck but would also result in her paying my firm excessive legal fees to dispute the bird cages. Put simply, if this could not be agreed, then the matter would remain in court. The cost in legal fees would surely outweigh the cost of the bird cages.

Another recent example is my office assisting a client to try to resolve his property settlement matter at an informal mediation conference. My client and his ex-partner were not able to resolve their overall property division because their negotiations became fixed and stuck on negotiating who would retain the splades. What is a splade, you ask?! It's a cross between a fork and a spoon. Certainly not of a value that would outweigh the ongoing expense of using lawyers.

 *Ask yourself: Is the battle going to cost more in legal fees than the desired outcome? If so, is it worth it?*

Remember the judgment of Justice Benjamin that I spoke about earlier in the book (his criticism of lawyers and the couple who collectively spent $860k on legal fees)? His Honour's judgment also made reference to the pages and pages of letters and correspondence in that matter – many of which he had read because they had been attached to court material. He said: *'Some of those letters were inflammatory and reflected the anger of the parties or one of them. The letters were at times accusatory. They were often verbose and at times involved unnecessary tit for tat commentary. Some of the letters served little or no forensic purposes.'*

Justice Benjamin made further comment in his judgment:

'Solicitors are not employed to act as "postman" to vent the anger and vitriol of their clients.'

Is your lawyer advising you on these issues and giving you ongoing support around whether correspondence is appropriate or even necessary? If your lawyer is simply doing whatever you want and you are venting, then you are likely spending unnecessary monies on legal fees.

Remember what we spoke about in Chapters 4 and 8 in relation to putting on your 'business hat'. This is particularly applicable when it comes to choosing your battles and ascertaining what is important to you.

 *Remember, your lawyer is not your puppet. You should be receiving clear advice around what correspondence and work is necessary and which is emotionally charged and unnecessary.*

Continue to communicate with your ex

How is your communication with your ex-partner? Is it relatively amicable? Do you have concerns for your safety or is there a power imbalance? In some circumstances, it might be appropriate to catch up with your ex-partner or keep the dialogue open, even if you both have solicitors. This can encourage a more speedy resolution.

If you decide to communicate with your ex-partner, then please *do not* show them copies of any correspondence or written advice that your lawyer has sent to you, and do not show them any draft documents which are not intended for them until finalised. It is positive that you would like to keep the lines of communication open with your ex-partner; however, you also need to protect your position (whether it be financial or in relation to parenting matters).

As I mentioned in Chapter 4, also be mindful that anything you write to your ex-partner via email or SMS or social media – and that is not written through lawyers – is not done on a 'without prejudice' basis, meaning that it may find its way annexed to a court affidavit if your matter ends up in court. As lawyers, we often draft correspondence and offers on a without prejudice basis, meaning that the other party is precluded from revealing the same to the court. This protects our clients while opening up the negotiation, and it does not lock our client into a position if we have to go to court.

Unfortunately, I have seen hundreds, if not thousands of examples of inappropriate communication and use of social media over the years. Derogatory or bullying SMS messages can be attached to an affidavit or to legal correspondence. They certainly will not help to reach an amicable agreement on anything. Denigration of your ex-partner on any social media platform is also a big *no no*. This can be particularly harmful in parenting matters. I have seen people post on social media in relation to court proceedings or just generally denigrate their ex-partner. The screenshots end up before the court or attached to legal correspondence. I can inform you that, as a lawyer, I absolutely Google the name of my client's ex-partner and search their social channels. If there is anything inappropriate, then I will screenshot that information before drawing it to my client's attention to request that it is removed. Follow the general rule of thumb, which we all learnt from our parents: 'If you've got nothing good to say, then don't say anything at all!'

 *Continue to communicate with your ex-partner if possible, but ensure what you say to and share with them is appropriate.*

I suggest focusing on communication with your ex-partner in relation to the 'smaller' decisions. These are the sorts of things that you may include in a Communication Book that exchanges at handover if you have children. Do you really need your lawyer to write to the other party about children's extra-curricular issues or particular issues in relation to schooling? Sometimes, you absolutely will need that support from your lawyer, but again this comes back to choosing your battles.

Sometimes, I have been pleasantly surprised when a client and their ex-partner have been able to meet and discuss various issues around their matter. It may be that they cannot agree on everything and still require legal assistance, but if it is possible to meet for coffee and have a chat about certain things, then why wouldn't you?

I recently had a client report to me that she and her ex-husband had gone for coffee and were able to resolve most of their parenting matter in an amicable way. This was a huge relief for her and also made my assistance with her property division much easier because we could focus on more difficult legal issues. Their amicable meeting and opening of communication showed good faith and went a long way to assist resolution of all other issues.

Paralegal & administrative input

Does your law firm have good support staff? The advantage of a good paralegal cannot be underestimated. They generally have law degrees or are studying law and are engaged by the firm to conduct practical work. They are not able to provide legal advice.

If you refer to your cost agreement (if you are not on a fixed-fee cost agreement), you will see that the rate of a non-lawyer (paralegal or administrative staff) can be half the cost of a lawyer providing the same service. You may be able to request that a paralegal assist with drafting documents or inspection of documents. You may request that the paralegal do any job on your file that does not require a solicitor, such as simple telephone calls.

I recommend transparency with your law firm in this respect and if they are not prepared to fix your legal fees, ask what services their paralegal can provide.

Many law firms have gems of secretaries and paralegals who can answer non-legal questions for you. They can provide procedural information and are sometimes across the procedural information more than the senior lawyers may be.

If you can develop relationships with these people, then you may be able to make them your first port of call. This alone can save you thousands of dollars.

TIPS – GET THE MOST OUT OF YOUR LAWYER:

- *Communicate effectively – if you are not on a fixed-fee plan, choose email over telephone or face-to-face communications where possible.*
- *Pick your battles – is what you're fighting for worth the cost?*
- *Ensure you have a lawyer who will advise you against unnecessary and/or inflammatory communications.*
- *Where possible, keep lines of communication open with your ex-partner, but protect your position – watch what you say to and share with them.*
- *Ask your law firm what services can be provided by their paralegal to keep your costs down.*

13

Ditching your lawyer!

IT IS NOT UNCOMMON FOR ME TO BE APPROACHED BY PEOPLE who are unhappy with their current lawyers – this is particularly common in the Family Law jurisdiction.

You are entitled to engage another lawyer if you are unhappy with your representation. That said, difficulties in changing lawyers may arise if you have outstanding legal fees, as it is then unlikely your complete file will be released to you. If you are on a deferred-fee cost agreement, then you will likely have signed an Irrevocable Authority, which the new firm will need to take into account.

Whether you change lawyers also depends on what stage you are at in the proceedings. Is it early days? Has much work has been done? How many hours will it take a new lawyer to get across all of the issues? Will the new lawyer need to re-read everything to get up to speed? You will likely need to pay any subsequent lawyer to read your file and also provide them with your instructions, which is likely to feel quite repetitive for you. This process can be costly but sometimes it is worthwhile. It really depends on your level of unhappiness and what stage your matter is at. If your matter is close to finalising, then consider whether it would be worthwhile changing representation at this point. If, however, you are still very much in the initial stages, then it may be a good time to change lawyers before you get too far in terms of time and money spent.

I once had a client who had spent over $30k at another private law firm come across to my firm. Given the amount of money spent, I was expecting boxes of files to follow. To my surprise, it turned out the previous lawyer had only conducted the matter for a few months, but had still managed to generate these significant fees. I suspect that the client in these circumstances did the right thing in changing firms. If she had continued as she was, then she would certainly have spent in excess of $100k.

If you are seriously thinking about changing lawyers, then *please*, before doing so, go back and read Chapter 5 on finding a lawyer. You should attend a meeting with the potential new lawyer to ensure that you want to instruct them. Out of professional courtesy and obligation, they will not provide any advice prior to you instructing their firm, but you will certainly get a feel for their legal knowledge and your confidence in them by discussing your matter broadly.

Meet with other potential lawyers before you ditch your current lawyer and ask about the potential costs and consequences of switching.

Questioning legal fees

If you are unhappy with your legal fees, then the first thing to do is refer to any cost agreement you have in place.

It is reasonable to ask your lawyer/law firm about what you are being billed. Consider the following:

- Ensure that you are provided with invoices. If you are not on a fixed-fee cost agreement, then there should be an itemised bill setting out each charge and all of the work completed.

- Ask specific questions that you may have about any item on your invoice.

- Ask to negotiate any fees you have been charged as well as any ongoing cost agreement or fees.

- Request more regular invoices so as to avoid bill shock.

- Ask for a 'heads-up' and to be notified when costs reach a certain amount.

- Ask how to dispute the invoice or any items on the invoice.

Each state has a complaint body that you can approach if you are unable to resolve any questions in relation to your legal fees or disputes in relation to invoices. Remember, Justice Benjamin referred his matter to the relevant complaint body in New South Wales for them to make an independent assessment. Lawyers have an obligation to respond to any complaint by or enquiry from these bodies.

You can apply for a cost assessment and/or for your cost agreement to be set aside and you can make a complaint for overcharging. There are generally time limitations when making an application for assessment.

The reality is that for small law firms and sole legal practitioners, it can be terrifying to receive a letter from the complaint body. It is very time-consuming to respond and smaller firms may not have the resources or time to deal with complaints. Larger firms may have the resources but may take the approach that smaller amounts in dispute would be easier for them to 'write off'.

 *If you have any concerns about costs, then I would always recommend speaking with your lawyer (or ex-lawyer) in the first instance.*

Stop! Before you change lawyers or go self-rep...

You are entitled to change lawyers at any stage. You are also able to cease instructing a lawyer and take over your matter on a self-represented basis. You are not required to continue to instruct your lawyer until the end of your settlement, agreement or court proceedings. But before ditching your lawyer, I encourage you to think of two things:

- What stage is your matter at?

- What are the real issues with your lawyer? Are they communication issues that can be resolved?

If your matter is close to completion, then changing lawyers or going self-represented may not be financially worthwhile. Keep in mind that any new lawyer will need to get up to speed with your matter and will likely spend hours reading and understanding your file. If your matter is due to be finalised shortly, then you should factor in the cost of changing lawyers – it may be better to stick it out.

Is your concern about the communication with your current lawyer as opposed to their conduct or the work they are undertaking? One of the most common complaints received by legal complaints bodies in Australia is in relation to unclear communication. Consider whether a transparent conversation with your legal team will address these concerns. Often, voicing such concerns or threatening to move your file to another firm is sufficient to get action.

STOP. Before changing lawyers, remember to consider what stage your matter is at and also whether a transparent conversation with your legal team could alleviate your concerns. The latter can go a long way towards addressing the issues.

Don't go MIA!

If you have not communicated to your lawyer that you are no longer instructing them, they will likely continue to charge you for work completed. You do not know what work they may be doing behind the scenes. This could include drafting documents, which can be expensive.

If you stop taking your lawyer's calls or responding to their emails, they may charge you for repeated attempts to get in touch with you. (Side note: If you have simply changed your address or contact details, then be sure to notify your law firm's administration team. Otherwise you may be charged for unnecessary, ongoing chase-up.)

I have seen many clients come across to my law firm after becoming dissatisfied with their previous lawyer. Some failed to properly advise their previous lawyer that they were leaving. The previous law firm continued to draft documents and letters in their matter and were entitled to be paid for the work that they had continued to do. That lawyer had no idea that their client no longer wanted to instruct them. My advice to anyone who has decided to change lawyers or who has decided to proceed on a self-represented basis is to confirm with your lawyer that you no longer want to instruct them and you do not want them to conduct any further work in your matter. A short email usually does the trick. If you had a relatively good working relationship with the law firm, then also pick up the phone and give them a courtesy call (or at least call to draw their attention to any email that you have sent ceasing your instructions).

Remember, if you do decide to proceed on a self-represented basis or if you do change lawyers, you are still ultimately required to pay your previous legal fees. The law firm is usually not required to release your file to you (or your new lawyer, if you have one) until your fees are settled. If you were previously on a deferred-fee cost agreement, then you may find that the law firm issues some form of debt collection or a charge is put on your property title. There may be interest payable for any late fees. It is best to understand the ramifications prior to leaving. Every matter will differ and will be subject to the particular cost agreement you have with that law firm. It will also depend on your relationship with the firm. If, for example, you decide to go self-represented but have a good relationship with your previous lawyer, they may allow you to enter a payment plan and/or avoid debt collection if you reach some sort of agreement with them.

TIPS – DITCHING YOUR LAWYER!

- *If you are unhappy with your legal fees, consult your cost agreement and question your invoices.*
- *Remember, you can go to a complaint body and apply for a cost assessment and/or for your cost agreement to be set aside and you can make a complaint for overcharging.*
- *But go to your lawyer first – threatening to switch to another lawyer or make a complaint may prompt action on your issue.*
- *What stage is your matter at? It may be better, cost-wise, to stick it out.*
- *Don't go MIA – if you are ditching your lawyer, inform them.*

14

Dealing with your ex-partner's lawyer

You do not have control over whether your ex-partner is self-represented or instructs an aggressive lawyer. Either way, it is recommended that you try to remain calm at all times. Keeping your cool throughout the process is likely to reduce your legal fees.

Whether you're dealing with an honest lawyer or an unscrupulous one, you still need to take care. I find that if I am communicating and negotiating with a self-represented party, I can 'get away' with a bit more than if I were dealing directly with another lawyer. This may include things such as negotiating a parenting agreement that is more favourable for my client or agreeing on values of property which are advantageous for my client's financial settlement. It may be that if the other party were represented, their lawyer would advise them against using certain values or reaching certain parenting agreements, but because they are not familiar with the Family Law, they are at a bit of a disadvantage. My obligation is to get the best outcome and results for my client, not to worry that their ex-partner is not well informed.

If your ex-partner has instructed a lawyer, then I recommend you read this chapter and take on board the tips for dealing and communicating with that lawyer. There are several 'dirty divorce tricks' that lawyers can employ, and it's best to be forewarned. Even if you wouldn't expect your ex-partner to resort to these tricks, it's worth knowing what the unscrupulous can get up to in order to protect yourself.

Understanding the opposing lawyer & complaints

So you're self-represented and navigating the Family Law space yourself. Unfortunately, you're in a position where you are dealing with your ex-partner's lawyer. Depending on communications with your ex-partner, that may or *may not* be a good thing! In some circumstances, it certainly may feel preferable to be communicating with your ex-partner's lawyer than your ex-partner themselves.

Lawyers are notorious for using legalese and may appear aggressive in their correspondence even if they do not intend to. I often ask a new client how their ex-partner will respond when receiving a letter for the first time from my law firm, because it is never ever pleasant to open an email or letter with a letterhead from a law firm. In many cases, it is appropriate to give your ex-partner the courtesy heads-up that they can anticipate receiving mail – particularly if you wish to maintain an amicable working relationship.

But what do you do if the lawyer your ex-partner has instructed seems to be using some of the dirty tricks I have referred to in this book or they simply do not seem focused on resolving your matter efficiently?

I spoke earlier about some of the tactics used by lawyers, and an important starting point when you are self-represented and dealing with a lawyer directly is to be mindful of these tactics. They can include:

- The overuse of legalese and legal jargon
- Unnecessary or lengthy correspondence
- Unnecessary and time-consuming document exchange
- Unnecessary applications in court
- 'Burning off' – essentially a weapon used to drag out your legal matter

You can read more about tactics employed by lawyers in Chapter 27, in relation to court proceedings.

But be aware, some of the above conduct may not be a deliberate tactic employed by the lawyer in order to challenge you. Bear in mind the legal profession is extremely conservative and the law has traditionally been difficult for the lay person to access or understand. There are many decent and well-meaning lawyers out there who continue to use a very traditional method of service delivery.

Keep in mind that just because you receive correspondence from a lawyer that seems very formal or contains legalese, it is not necessarily a reflection on your ex-partner but rather the way that a lawyer has been traditionally trained to do their job. At other times, it may in fact be a deliberate tactic used to demonstrate the lawyer's knowledge or to establish a power imbalance, given you are self-represented and may have trouble understanding the jargon.

 **You are likely to receive correspondence from lawyers full of legalese, which may come across as dismissive of you or even aggressive. Try to remain focused, put on your business hat and treat things as a commercial transaction.**

Don't be tempted to engage or become responsive if you think dirty tactics are being deployed. Try to resist the temptation of writing long or unnecessary correspondence or documents just because your ex-partner's lawyer has. If you feel as though your ex-partner is filing applications in court which are simply to put pressure on you or that do not have merit, get some legal advice in relation to those applications and whether it is appropriate to seek a cost order against your ex-partner.

This is also a time when it is imperative that your communications with your ex-partner's lawyer are civil and businesslike. In my work as an independent children's lawyer, I work with many families who do not have lawyers and who are doing their best to represent themselves in court. Many of these parties are professional people; however, their conduct during court hearings and the emotion and anger that they express in correspondence and court documents are far from how they would conduct themselves in a business setting. Family Law and separation are highly emotive, and all too frequently I see people who are representing themselves let off steam at inappropriate times. Going off on rants or becoming defensive or aggressive is unlikely to assist you to progress your matter.

Remember, the role of that lawyer is to represent your ex-partner's interests and act on their instructions, not yours. You can anticipate that the legal practitioner for your ex-partner will say things and write things that you disagree with and make statements that are not in your interest.

One tip is to try to manage your emotions as well as you can and remember that you cannot control your ex-partner's lawyer. You can only control what you can control.

Remember that your ex-partner's lawyer has an obligation to keep their client informed and to provide your ex-partner with all of your correspondence, documents and offers to resolve your matter. I recommend being civil and respectful in your communications and remaining aware that they are being read by your ex-partner as well as their lawyer.

TIPS – DEALING WITH YOUR EX-PARTNER'S LAWYER:

- *Keep your cool at all times.*
- *Be mindful of the tactics a lawyer may employ.*
- *Do not respond in kind if you think dirty tactics are being used.*

- *Obtain legal advice about whether a cost order could be sought if you think your ex is filing unnecessary applications in court.*
- *Remain focused and remember to put on your business hat.*

PART THREE:
DIVORCE

15

DIY divorce

As mentioned earlier, a divorce application is very much a separate issue to resolving your property and/or parenting matter. If you were not married to your partner, then you will not need to read this part of the book.

Thankfully, since 1976, Australia has operated a 'no fault' divorce system. Gone are the days of detectives trying to catch your spouse committing adultery!

'No fault' implies exactly that. It is irrelevant if one of you was having an affair. It does not matter whether your conduct or your ex-partner's conduct caused the relationship to break down. When applying for a divorce, no reason needs to be given. Put simply, the court does not care about why your marriage broke down.

I often tell clients that it takes the consent of both parties to enter into a marriage; however, only one person needs to make the decision to separate. You may be surprised at the number of new clients I speak with who are unhappy about the separation and do not 'consent' to either the separation or divorce.

If one spouse does not want to proceed with the divorce, then there is nothing precluding the other party from proceeding with their court application for divorce by themselves with a sole application. Only one party is required to apply for a divorce and it does not require the consent of both spouses.

I need to be clear that it is not a legal requirement to apply for a divorce unless you intend to remarry. I suspect, given you have purchased this book, that you are in the early stages of your separation and it is unlikely that you are considering re-marriage at this point! But this is something to bear in mind.

Some of my clients are keen to divorce as soon as they are legally able to because they want that emotional closure or disconnection from their spouse. Other clients just never get around to it and it is not important to them from an emotional point of view. The important thing to remember here is your property settlement time limits. If you have property to be divided in your marriage, then re-read the sections in this book in relation to property settlements and time limits. There are many clients whom I advise to delay their divorce application because it provides us more time to try to resolve their property matter without the time limitations causing problems. With other clients, I advise them to apply for a divorce as soon as possible so that the time limitation commences and it acts as a means to protect their assets. Every matter is different.

DIY divorce

Divorce is one area of Family Law where you really should consider doing it yourself. The court forms are relatively simple and the Family Law Court even publishes a DIY Divorce Kit.

 **Want the link to the Family Law Court DIY Kit? Feel free to send my office an email (lawyers@familylawproject.com.au) and we will email the kit to you.**

If you have ever been to the Family Law Court on a Divorce List day, you will have noticed that it is not uncommon to have upwards of fifty matters listed over the course of the morning. Crazy, right?! If you pop your head into the courtroom (it is an open court, meaning that any adult can observe), then you will also note the number of self-represented litigants. There are generally more people attending without lawyers than with lawyers.

There may be a bit of waiting around involved, given the number of matters, and if you can't take the time or you cannot take time off work, then that is when you should consider instructing a lawyer. Otherwise you're likely to be more than capable of appearing in court yourself. The hearing is before a registrar (a lower-level official than a judge), who is generally not intimidating, and the hearing is less formal than, say, a parenting or property matter. The registrar will only spend up to five minutes on your matter and the questions they ask you will be quite easy.

Some law firms will charge thousands for completing your divorce application and appearing before the registrar. I frequently provide the Divorce Kit to clients, recommending they DIY divorce and spend the saved money elsewhere. If I am acting for a client in relation to their parenting and/or property matter, then I suggest that their money is better applied towards those legal fees.

Divorce applications are 'money for jam' for lawyers! If your matter is standard, then my strong advice is to DIY divorce.

 *DIY divorce – this is one area of Family Law which is relatively easy to navigate without a lawyer.*

Divorce applications

YOU NEED TO CONSIDER WHETHER TO MAKE A JOINT OR SOLE application for divorce. This really depends on your particular circumstances and your level of communication, if any, with your ex-spouse.

At the time of writing, the court filing fee for a divorce application is a hefty $865. The reduced fee for someone who meets the means test is $290. You will qualify for the reduced concession rate if you hold a Health Care Card or any Centrelink concession card. If there is a joint application, then you *both* must qualify for the reduction. If your ex-partner qualifies for the reduced rate but is not taking any steps to apply for a divorce, then you may want to encourage them to apply and then pay them the reduced-cost filing fee. Alternatively, you may want to negotiate with your ex-partner how to pay the filing fee if neither of you qualify for the reduced amount.

Take advantage of the reduced filing fee if one or both of you qualify. If only your ex-partner qualifies, consider offering to pay the reduced fee to encourage them to file.

Service

Any sole application for divorce will need to be 'served' on the other party. The court needs to be satisfied that the other party has received the documents and is aware of the proceedings. A divorce order will not be granted on a sole application where you cannot establish that there has been adequate service.

While we frequently use process servers to serve documents, you may want to consider using an independent friend or family member over the age of eighteen to serve the application on your ex-partner. This will likely save you $150+ in service fees. The friend or family member will need to complete an Affidavit of Service document, which essentially sets out the date and time that your ex-spouse was served. This document can be witnessed by a Justice of the Peace and is filed with the court. The court even has a service kit which sets out how to go about personally serving your ex-spouse, which I recommend you have a look at.

Have an independent friend or family member serve the application to avoid paying a process server.

Reasons to apply for a divorce

Aside from the desire to remarry, there can be legal advantages to applying for a divorce. It may be financially wise for you to fork out the $865 filing fee as a means of protecting your financial interests.

The reason for this essentially comes down to the rule which stipulates that both parties only have twelve months from the date of a divorce order to negotiate or initiate proceedings for property division. Once the twelve-month limitation has lapsed, then it can be extremely difficult to apply to the court for division of property. I have advised many clients who are the main asset holder at separation, in that either the family home, investment property, superannuation or other main assets are in their sole name. In effect, once the twelve-month limitation has lapsed, those assets will remain in the sole name of the holder, with the ex-spouse having no entitlement to claim them or a share of them.

The above is an example of a valuable piece of advice that I frequently give to clients in a free first meeting or during the initial stages of advice. Never underestimate how much you can save by obtaining even some limited advice from a Family Law specialist. Very often, I will advise these clients to proceed with the divorce application as soon as they are able and then quietly sit back, cross their fingers and hope for twelve-plus months to pass. This is particularly apt where there may be limited assets, perhaps only superannuation, and the other party does not get around to obtaining legal advice or does not pursue a superannuation splitting order. Legal advice to do nothing can be valuable!

Some clients wish to pursue a divorce order for emotional closure, which is also completely understandable.

 *It may be in your interest to fork out the $865 filing fee to speed up the time limitation process with the*

> *hope that your ex-spouse has difficulty making a future claim on property and assets in your sole name.*

Complex divorce applications

Not all divorce applications are simple.

You may need to engage a lawyer if you do not know the whereabouts of your spouse. In order to bypass the requirement of service (as outlined above), the court needs to be satisfied that you have made *all reasonable attempts* to locate your spouse. A simple Facebook search will not cut it and there are other means to attempt and searches that should be conducted and outlined in an affidavit to be filed by the court.

Another example is where you and your spouse have separated but have remained living under the same roof. I worked as a Duty Lawyer at the Sydney and Parramatta Registries, and I often spoke to clients who had separated but who were living under the same roof purely for financial reasons. The cost of living in cities such as Sydney can be prohibitive, particularly if you are waiting for your matrimonial property settlement to be effected.

You are required to be separated for twelve months before you are allowed to file for a divorce. If you have been living together for all or part of that time, then you will also need to file an affidavit setting out the circumstances of the separation (i.e. sleeping in separate rooms, preparing your own meals, separate washing, not socialising as a couple, financial separation of bank accounts and assets, and so on). Sometimes, you will both need to file affidavits (in a joint application) and a third party may also need to swear an affidavit.

Although my office rarely prepares standard divorce applications, we will assist in these tricky divorce matters.

If you need to engage a lawyer to assist in a complex divorce, then you should ask to have your fees fixed. You could ask for a lawyer to draft your documents and provide legal advice, but then attend the court hearing yourself to save money.

Do not delay your property negotiations

You can commence your property division and negotiations immediately after separation. You do not need to wait until you apply for a divorce or until a divorce order is made.

Keep in mind that you generally only have twelve months from the date of the divorce order to resolve and/or initiate court proceedings with respect to your property division. Any delay in this respect could end up costing you thousands!

There is a common misconception that you need to wait for your divorce before dealing with your property; however, that is simply not true. In many cases, it is best to commence your property negotiations as soon as possible.

TIPS – DIVORCE APPLICATIONS:

- Take advantage of the reduced filing fee if you or your ex-partner qualifies for it.
- Avoid paying a process server by having an independent friend or family member serve the application.
- Be aware of the legal advantages of applying for a divorce. It may be worth forking out the filing fee to protect your financial interests.
- If you need a lawyer to help navigate a complex divorce, ask for a fixed fee. Remember, you could get them to prepare documents and provide advice but attend the court hearing by yourself.
- Keep time limits in mind – you generally only have twelve months from the date of the divorce order to resolve and/or initiate court proceedings with respect to your property division.

PART FOUR
PROPERTY

17

Property matters

IN ORDER FOR ME TO PROVIDE TIPS AND RECOMMENDATIONS around saving money in property settlement matters, it is necessary to give you a brief overview of what is involved when discussing a 'property settlement' and the various ways that a property settlement matter can be resolved.

In almost all cases, your matter is best resolved outside of court. There are always exceptions, however, such as when a matter is urgent, the other party is being deceitful or there is a lack of engagement from your ex-partner. In those matters, your hand is likely to be forced to initiate proceedings.

Trying to resolve your property settlement can be particularly difficult. The Australian Law Reform Commission recommended in 2019 that there should be a clear framework to guide the courts and public regarding the division of assets. The law and much of the process have not changed since then. It remains extremely difficult to navigate. Each matter is different, which, from a lawyer's perspective, can mean it's challenging to provide initial advice to clients.

The difficulty with trying to determine your property entitlement is that the law is discretionary. Some say that, with respect to petty disputes, the Australian Family Law system is one of the most *inconsistent* in the world and that **lawyers have a vested interest in maintaining the chaos!**

So, let's break things down.

What is a property settlement?

A property settlement is an agreement or a court order which sets out the division and dealings of all of the assets of the parties. It can provide a timeline for certain property to be transferred, for the sale of property, for superannuation to be divided and for cash payments.

A formal property settlement provides the parties with assurance when it comes to finality and the division of assets. It ensures that it is not left open for either party to seek further and 'better' division of assets at a later date.

Know your relationship type

It is important to understand your relationship type and what protections and obligations flow on from that relationship type.

A married couple is self-explanatory! A 'de facto' relationship may require more explanation. There were some significant changes to the legislation in Australia in 2008 which essentially resulted in de facto couples separating after 1 March 2009 (or 1 July 2010 in SA) being able to seek property adjustment orders pursuant to the *Family Law Act*. The Act sets out the threshold requirements to be able to make a claim for property division.

Importantly, as we discussed earlier in the book, the relationship must have existed for at least two years, but it is not enough to have simply been together for two years – you need to have been living together on a genuine domestic basis. The Act identifies not only the duration of the relationship but also other considerations, such as: whether there was a sexual relationship, whether you lived together, whether there was financial interdependence, whether property is owned in joint names and whether you would be considered a de facto couple by friends and family. The two-year period can be a continuous period or over stages.

If your relationship has not existed for at least two years, you can still qualify for property division if:

- You have a child;

- You made substantial contributions;

- The relationship was registered under a prescribed law in your state/territory; or

- It would result in a serious injustice if you were not allowed to seek a property settlement.

 *Don't think you were de facto or not quite sure? It's worth getting some legal advice to confirm either way – even in a free advice session from a Legal Aid office or a community legal centre. It may be in your interest to dispute the fact that there was ever a de facto relationship.*

First steps – the family home

It is difficult to commence negotiations for your property division or turn your mind to options for your property division until you have thought through what is important to you and what you ultimately want to achieve.

Do you wish to stay living in the family home? Do you want to move back into the home? Is the family home likely to be sold because neither of you can afford to refinance and take over the mortgage? These are things that you should immediately consider, particularly before you leave the family home. It can also help to determine who stays in the family home and who leaves.

If the property is held as a joint tenancy (i.e. both your name and your ex-partner's name are on the certificate of title), then technically you both are able to live at the property and come and go as you please. As mentioned in the divorce section of this book, it is not uncommon for couples to separate but remain living together under the same roof after separation because of the prohibitive cost of obtaining independent accommodation.

If you have children, then it is generally preferable for them to be able to remain in the family home. They have already faced major changes with their parents having separated, and if you can keep their housing and schooling arrangements consistent, then that is preferable.

If it is your intention to remain living in the property, then you should make immediate enquiries with a financial advisor or lender as to whether you are in a financial position to do so. Are you able to service the mortgage on your single income? How much are you able to refinance in the event that your ex-partner needs to be 'paid out' settlement monies? Ascertain what your borrowing capacity is to help you with your negotiations and know what is realistic.

You should make these enquiries before attempting to negotiate your property settlement. You will go into any negotiation with much more confidence if you know your borrowing capacity and know realistically what you can afford to pay out or how much money you need to purchase another property.

It is very difficult to begin the negotiation or mediation process if you do not yet have advice around your borrowing and refinancing capacity. I am surprised at the number of clients I assist who have remained living in the family home and ultimately want the property transferred to their sole name, yet they have not made the enquiry with a financial institution in relation to their borrowing capacity. In my view, it is one of the first things that you should seek advice about.

If you are considering asking your ex-partner to leave or if they refuse to leave and you need an order of the court for sole occupancy (more about that later), then knowing your borrowing capacity in those circumstances is also valuable. This is something that can be effected without a lawyer and certainly these enquiries should be made directly by you.

 *Know your borrowing capacity. How can you otherwise negotiate a property settlement?*

The other thing that you should discuss with your current financial institution is your capacity to meet the current mortgage repayments. Has your ex-partner ceased making financial contribution towards the mortgage? Can you afford to continue making repayments? If a mortgage is in joint names, then you both continue to be jointly liable for this debt. If you default in payments (for whatever reason), then it is likely to affect both your credit rating and borrowing capacity.

Perhaps it is all a bit too much at the moment, in the early days after separation. If so, it is not uncommon for a financial institution to approve a short-term suspension or break from your mortgage. Ensure that you understand all of the terms and conditions in doing so. You should also obtain independent financial advice. I suggest, if this is something that you seriously want to consider, that you make an appointment with your financial institution to discuss your personal circumstances.

 Get financial advice early.

Alternatively, is it likely that neither of you want to retain the family home? Is it ultimately going to be put on the market for sale? Some clients delay this process, thinking that they need to agree on the substantive overall property settlement first. Please note that there is nothing precluding you both from going ahead and putting the property on the market for sale.

If you do so, then:

- Jointly instruct a real estate agent and ensure that those instructions require you both to have input;

- Agree on the minimum sale price (to be instructed to the agent); and

- Jointly sign instructions to the real estate agent that any proceeds of sale are to remain in the conveyancer trust account, pending you both providing written consent.

This last point is really important. You don't want to put off the sale process and potentially miss a good buyer or sale price because you have not been able to agree on how the overall property is to be divided. A conveyancer can hold the proceeds of sale jointly for you in their trust account, with no one able to access the funds unless there is a written agreement for partial or full release of the monies. This option is great for some people, as it allows them to get on with finding a rental property or a new house or whatever their personal situation requires.

You and your ex-partner may agree to a partial release of funds to each party to help with your immediate financial needs; however, the residual stays put until you both instruct the conveyancer to release it. Alternatively, you can instruct that the proceeds sit in a joint interest-bearing bank account. Ensure the account requires joint signatures for any release of funds. This provides you with financial protection also. You may find that it also encourages and expedites an overall settlement, as it can be quite frustrating for both parties having monies held in a conveyancer trust account which cannot be accessed!

TIPS – PROPERTY MATTERS:

- *Do you know if you were in a de facto relationship? It's worth getting some legal advice to confirm your relationship status. You could discuss this in an advice session at a Legal Aid office or a community legal centre.*
- *Ensure you know your borrowing capability so you are in a position to negotiate your settlement.*
- *Seek financial advice early.*

Property settlement – the four-step process

There is a common misconception that property in Family Law matters is divided '50/50' when you separate. This is a myth.

So, what is considered when determining the property division?

If you do seek legal advice, you will hear lawyers talk about a 'four-step process'. Even if you are negotiating your matter with your ex-partner away from court and without lawyers, it is still important to consider this to see what would be considered if your matter were in court.

All mediation services and lawyers will use the four-step process and principles to work through issues around property division. Division of property matters can be a difficult process, as every matter is considerably different and there is no mathematical exercise to let us know immediately what the correct division would be. The process is set out in the *Family Law Act* and is a good starting point.

Below is a brief summary of the steps and considerations when negotiating your property division:

1. What is the asset pool?
This is the step where we consider all of the assets and liabilities at separation. It is irrelevant whether properties are held in sole or joint names – they all form part of the asset pool. I go into more detail about the asset pool in the next section.

2. What are the parties' contributions?
The contribution of each party needs to be considered. This factors in both financial and non-financial contributions. One party might have brought in significantly more assets at the commencement of the relationship, they might have received a large inheritance or they may have been the main 'bread winner'. These are financial contributions. Non-financial contributions include homemaking, improvements to the home, managing any investment properties and caring for children.

3. What are the parties' future needs and capacity?
Future needs and capacity are very important. This consideration centres on current and potential earnings and any future medical needs or incapacity. I often give my clients an example of imbalance – imagine one party is on a salary of $200k+ and their ex-partner is unemployed and in receipt of a Centrelink benefit. Clearly, one of these parties will be in a much better financial position moving forward. There will be consideration given to your employment, difficulties around employment capacity, the ongoing care of any children and the likelihood of payment of any child support.

4. Is the division just and equitable?

After considering all of the above, the final step when negotiating your property settlement (or consideration by the court if your matter is before the court) is to consider whether the division would be just and equitable.

Determining whether the property settlement is just and equitable is a difficult step to navigate. It really is dependent on the circumstances of each individual matter. There is no definitive list of circumstances that I can provide for you to check what the just and equitable result in your matter might be.

When a matter is before the court, the judge will look at the proposed property settlement as a whole and the practical impact on each party to decide whether the proposed division is fair. The court has to consider the practical effect of the actual order itself and not just the underlying percentage of division of property. Are the proposed orders fair for both parties? An example is where the court allows a wife to forgo a large percentage of her superannuation calculated entitlement in exchange for a discounted cash sum payout with no superannuation adjustment. In this matter, the court would be considering the wife's need to rehouse and her need for funds to adequately provide for herself. Another example is where the court allows a husband a longer period of time to get his finances together to pay out the wife to enable him to maintain the family home rather than having to sell it.

The asset pool

When a de facto couple or married couple separate, more often than not there is property which is considered 'property of the relationship'. This may need to be divided. The first step is to ascertain exactly what the property pool consists of. You will need to consider all assets of the parties at the time of separation, inclusive of assets held in joint names and sole name.

The property that will need to be considered includes but is not limited to:

- The family home
- Any properties brought into the relationship by one party
- Any investment properties
- Shares
- Superannuation
- Savings in bank accounts
- Any businesses
- Motor vehicles
- Household contents

There are certain things to be aware of to help put you in the best possible financial position after separation, regardless of whether or not you are instructing a lawyer.

You need to start gathering all relevant information. I have already discussed the importance of keeping documentation organised in a separate folder and preferably electronically also. Again, think of this as a business transaction. The purpose of gathering information and supporting documentation is to agree the asset pool between the parties. It does not matter whether you are negotiating directly with your ex-partner, mediating at a family dispute resolution service or using lawyers; the first step should attempt to establish the asset pool.

Ideally, the value of assets should also be agreed between you. This is easier said than done. Often, formal valuations will be required if parties simply cannot agree on the values of the various assets.

You will also need to identify and value the liabilities of the relationship, which include but are not limited to:

- Any mortgages
- Any borrowings or loans
- HECS/HELP debts
- ATO debts
- Business debts
- Personal loans
- Credit cards and store cards

Once you have ascertained and valued the asset pool, the parties can move forward with their negotiation as to how much or what percentage each party will receive. Agreeing on the value of the pool in the first instance makes this negotiation easier.

I talk more about ways to value property further on.

Options to resolve your property settlement

You do not *need* to go to court to resolve your property settlement.

The more information gathering you can do yourself, the better. Your aim should be to agree on the asset pool with your ex-partner as soon as possible (or, alternatively, obtain valuations where required). Where possible, avoid initiating court proceedings. If this is suggested to you, then have your lawyer explain clearly why alternative options are not being used.

It can take time to gather all of the financial particulars and agree on the value of the asset pool. I am aware that many clients find this process particularly slow and frustrating. A fall-back option may be court; however, my view is that that should only be used if your ex-partner is being unreasonable in the negotiation process or has their 'head in the sand'.

Avoid court if you can. It should be possible to resolve most property matters without initiating court proceedings. Court will likely end up costing you more money and can be incredibly stressful.

The discovery process & disclosure

The Family Law rules require that both parties in a financial matter must provide what is called 'full and frank disclosure'. This means that you must provide your ex-partner (or their lawyer) with copies of all information relevant to your case. The documents can be exchanged in hard copy (i.e. paper) or electronically. Full and frank disclosure is required, even if you are negotiating with your ex-partner directly and are not using the court. The reason for this is so that you are both satisfied that you have each fully disclosed all of the current assets that you have an interest in.

Full disclosure is required so that you can confidently negotiate a property division. If it later transpires that either party held interest in property that was not disclosed, then it may be open to apply to the court for further property division on the grounds that assets were essentially hidden or not adequately disclosed.

Your obligation to exchange any relevant material is ongoing and it is important to remember that if you receive updated valuations or come across further monies or assets (inheritance, a work cover claim or lottery winnings, for example), then you have a continued obligation to disclose this to your ex-partner. If you have a lawyer and you provide them with copies of any appraisals or valuations, then we generally have an obligation to disclose them to the other party (even if you are unhappy with the values/figures).

 *Earlier in the book, I spoke about the importance of being as organised as possible. Aim to have all of your financial documents in order for your lawyer and/or your ex-partner.*

Having your financial documents in order will save you time later. If you do have a lawyer, it may also minimise your legal fees – your lawyer will not be spending time trying to work through and organise the documents for you.

The types of documents that you will be expected to exchange with your ex-partner, whether or not you are legally represented, include:

- Confirmation of income (your three most recent tax assessments and payslips)

- Superannuation statements

- Bank and mortgage statements

- Statements and valuations for all property and all financial resources

The obligation extends to the year prior to separation in that you need to disclose documents in relation to earnings, savings, and disposal or acquisition of any property during that time. There may be other key dates that are relevant to your particular matter and if your ex-partner asks for specific information, then you need to provide it if relevant.

Bad behaviour

I have seen all sorts of bad behaviour from both my clients and opposing parties over my years working as a family lawyer. Examples of bad behaviour in the discovery process include:

- Hiding money

- Not disclosing assets

- Intentionally becoming underemployed or unemployed post separation

- The small business owner who has been cooking the books prior to separation or post separation (or both)

- Deliberate depletion of the asset pool post separation

It can be really difficult to provide advice in this situation because, often, the value of the hidden asset or hidden profits of a business are unknown. The amount of depletion of the asset pool may be unknown or hard to prove. The reckless or negligent depletion of the asset pool without your knowledge or consent is not allowed, but it can also be difficult to prove. There are options, such as forensic examination of businesses and finances, but frankly that can cost thousands of dollars. Sometimes, the cost of that process outweighs any finding.

Sometimes, we see someone try to tweak their current financial position to impact the 'future needs' adjustment of the asset pool (i.e. so that they are seen to need an adjustment of the property pool favourable to them to take into account their difficult financial position). If your ex-partner has conveniently found their business profits have significantly reduced after separation or they are now unemployed, we are able to consider their profit and employment history through the discovery process. This is one of the reasons the exchange of documents such as ATO and bank statements is important. It is often obvious if there has been a long-standing history of employment but now a questionable unemployment.

TIPS – PROPERTY SETTLEMENT:

- *Avoid court if at all possible. Initiating court proceedings over property can be very costly.*
- *Be organised – have all your documents in order to share with your lawyer and/or ex-partner.*

Valuing the property pool

ANY ATTEMPT THAT YOU CAN MAKE YOURSELF TO GATHER information and obtain supporting documents, independent of your solicitor, will save you money. If you are self-represented, then having values at hand means they can be exchanged with your ex-partner or their lawyer when necessary. This can expedite the negotiation process.

There is no legal requirement for you to obtain valuations or appraisals of all of the property pool if you and your ex-partner can agree on values. In some circumstances, it may be in your interest not to proceed with a valuation or appraisal if your ex-partner is agreeing to a value that is favourable to you.

 *Even if you are legally represented, you can still make enquiries and gather appraisals and valuations yourself rather than instructing your lawyer to do so.*

Real estate

How much is the family home worth? How about that investment property? The property market in Australia is unpredictable and property prices can certainly fluctuate over time, particularly if you take a couple of years to resolve your property division. If you do have a lawyer, remember that they are not a real estate agent or a property valuer and are not experienced enough to be giving advice as to the value of property. Likewise, if you are dealing with your ex-partner directly, you also cannot with confidence agree on any value that they place on the property.

Many clients inform me of the value the council assigns to the property via the council rate notices. In almost all cases, the council valuation is not reflective of the actual market price. It usually represents a lower amount than the actual value. Likewise, as a general rule, bank valuations are not usually indicative of the value of the property. Your bank or financial institution may value the property for the purpose of refinancing but, ultimately, they want to protect their interest and equity in the property in the event that you default on your mortgage repayments. But as I've mentioned, there is no need to obtain any formal valuations if you and your ex-partner agree on the value of the property. If you are staying in the family home or retaining the investment property and your ex agrees to use the council rate as the 'agreed value', then it may be in your interest to use that figure if it subsequently means you are required to pay out less in settlement monies.

 *If your ex-partner agrees on a value for property that is favourable to you, then there is no need*

to have the property formally valued. Parties are able to agree on any value for the purpose of negotiation.

I suspect if your ex-partner receives legal advice that they may be advised not to agree on figures favourable to you, but it is worthwhile keeping in mind.

Valuations of property by a registered valuer will generally cost $500 to $1,000. If this cost is prohibitive or if your ex-partner will not agree to share in the cost of a valuation, then you may wish to obtain three appraisals from real estate agents and agree to consider the median value of the three. A valuation by a registered valuer will hold more weight in negotiations (and be much more likely to be considered if your matter ever gets to court) as opposed to the appraisals. If your matter ends up in court and you cannot agree on the value of real estate, then an order will likely be made for the parties to jointly obtain a formal valuation.

 *If you cannot afford to obtain a valuation of the property from a registered valuer, then obtain three free appraisals from real estate agents.*

Motor vehicle valuations

When determining the asset pool, you will need to take into consideration any motor vehicles, motorbikes and caravans. The website Redbook is a lawyer's 'go to' website to ascertain these values. The website enables you to provide details in relation to make, model, year and condition of the car. You can also purchase reports at an additional expense, but that is not generally necessary in the first instance.

I recommend that you make your own Redbook enquiries for any of these assets, regardless of whether they are in your sole name, your ex's sole name or in joint names.

If you have a lawyer, then you can gather this information for them to save you from paying for their time to obtain it for you.

 **You can make the enquiries here: redbook.com.au**

Furniture & personal belongings

The reality is that most of my clients overestimate the value of their household contents and personal effects, regardless of whether they have remained in the property or they have left the family home.

Most people want to avoid having a formal valuation of household contents and furniture. When lawyers negotiate a property settlement and also when a matter is before the court, the value of these assets is based on the second-hand value of the belongings. For example, what would these items fetch on a website such as gumtree.com.au?

Unless you have expensive antique pieces, artwork or new electronic goods (such as the latest mega TV), it is very easy to overestimate the value of your household contents. An insurance value is also unlikely to be an accurate reflection for Family Law purposes, as it is also likely to be higher.

Having said that, if there are expensive tools or other items, then there is merit to itemising them. I assisted a client whose ex-partner had a number of magnum bottles of Penfolds Grange and he was minimising their value. A simple wine search indicated their combined current value was around $6,000, so they certainly should have been itemised.

The point is not to get stuck in negotiating and itemising every single item including your Tupperware! The sad reality is that for one person (generally the person who has left the family home), it can be costly to start again. The cost of setting up a new home in terms of all the small bits and pieces is rarely taken into account from a Family Law perspective.

If you have a lawyer, then, depending on a realistic value, you do not want to be spending hundreds or even thousands of dollars negotiating the cost of household contents. I am often consulted by clients who have left the family home and had to set up again, and they can find this particularly difficult given the cost of buying new furniture and household goods.

Unless your household items are particularly valuable, do not waste too much time or energy negotiating their value. In particular, do not instruct a lawyer for ongoing negotiations in relation to contents if, realistically, the value is minimal. Remember to pick your battles!

Superannuation

We are frequently asked about superannuation and whether or not it falls within the asset pool. The short answer is 'yes'.

While it is considered an asset of the property pool, whether it is divided will depend on many factors in your individual circumstances, such as:

- The length of your relationship
- The total value of the asset pool
- The future financial capacity of each party
- The superannuation entitlement of the other party

There is no automatic presumption that both parties' superannuation will be split or that your ex-partner will receive half of your superannuation. Again, that is another common misconception that we hear frequently.

The Family Law Legislation Amendment (Superannuation) Act 2001 came into effect in 2002. This now makes it possible for superannuation to be split if the amount to be split is over $5,000. The amendment to the legislation makes it very clear that superannuation is considered property and forms part of the overall asset pool. The legislation was initially for married couples only, but now has been rolled out to include de facto couples in all states except for Western Australia. Having said that, WA looks set to be allowing the change also. It does seem unfair that someone's postcode can prevent superannuation from being split!

Prior to the amendments, being unable to split superannuation was often unfair for one party.

Consider the following:

- The asset pool is nominal, aside from the family home (with very little equity) and superannuation owned by Party X. Party X wishes to stay in the family home with the children; however, given their superannuation is so high, they are assessed as having to make a cash payout to party Y. They cannot afford to refinance, meaning the family home has to be sold.

- The only asset of the relationship is the very large superannuation benefit belonging to Party X. If the superannuation cannot be split, then Party Y will not receive any of the assets.

The changes to the legislation are aimed at protecting vulnerable parties and also those parties who have a large amount of superannuation, by enabling them to transfer a base amount of superannuation to the other party rather than refinancing to pay the other party a cash amount.

If you are negotiating your property settlement with your ex-partner, then you will need to exchange superannuation statements. Ideally, you should exchange statements as at the date of separation and also the most recent statement for all trustees. If it looks as though there may be a superannuation splitting agreement, then you will need to make what is called a Form 6 Family Law enquiry with the superannuation trustee and also accord them procedural fairness once the agreement has been reached. Procedural fairness means that they have been provided with a copy of the draft agreement and have approved that agreement.

A Form 6 enquiry can be made since changes to the legislation were made. It requires the trustee to set out the value of the superannuation as at certain dates. The good thing about a Form 6 enquiry is that it can be made by a non-member spouse at any time. A non-member 'spouse' includes a de facto partner. If you would like clarification as to the value of your ex-partner's superannuation, then you can make this Form 6 enquiry at any stage before or after separation. The beauty of this enquiry is that the legislation requires the trustee to keep the enquiry confidential. They cannot tell their member (your ex-partner) that such an enquiry has been made. This is a good way to ascertain how much superannuation your ex-partner has if they are not being transparent with you.

If you have a lawyer, they will likely arrange a Form 6 valuation for you if it seems as though there will be superannuation splitting or if your ex-partner is not engaging in the negotiation process. You can contact the trustee directly and generally obtain their Form 6 request on their website. The administration fee will need to be paid, but it will be nominal. If you make this enquiry instead of your solicitor, then this is another way to save in legal fees.

Form 6 enquiry needed? You can make arrangements to do this yourself without a lawyer. If you have a lawyer, you can still do this yourself

and provide them with the information once you have obtained it.

If there is any agreement for superannuation splitting, then it needs to be drafted correctly in the format of either consent minutes of order or a binding financial agreement. The wording is very precise and needs to be approved by the superannuation trustee.

If you are considering the best area in which to engage a lawyer, then the drafting of the property agreement is important because the superannuation split cannot be done without the consent minutes of order or a binding financial agreement.

If you are considering superannuation splitting as part or all of your overall property settlement, then be mindful that you cannot access it as a cash withdrawal unless approved by the trustee.

Approval will almost certainly mean that you meet their grounds of financial hardship. The threshold for compassionate release on the grounds of financial hardship is usually very high.

In most cases, you will not be able to access the superannuation until your ex-partner retires. How practical will superannuation splitting be for you? Do you need access to money immediately? Consider these factors before agreeing to any superannuation split.

TIPS – PROPERTY SETTLEMENT:

- *To save costs, gather appraisals and valuations yourself rather than instructing your lawyer to do so.*
- *There is no need to seek a formal valuation if you and your ex-partner can agree on the value of items.*
- *Obtain three free appraisals from real estate agents if you cannot afford to obtain a valuation of the property from a registered valuer.*
- *Make enquiries about motor vehicle valuations at: redbook.com.au*
- *Pick your battles! Do not waste too much time negotiating values unless there are items of very high value involved.*
- *You can complete a Form 6 enquiry regarding superannuation yourself, rather than have your lawyer do it. This is kept confidential by the trustee.*
- *The best area in which to engage a lawyer would be the drafting of the property agreement, since superannuation cannot be split without consent minutes of order or a binding financial agreement.*

20

Property division – urgent matters

You may be trying to avoid using a lawyer (or at least keep your legal fees to a minimum); however, there are some circumstances where I suggest you seek urgent legal advice:

- If you need urgent access to income/money and the funds have been cut off.

- If you require an urgent spousal maintenance order because you are in a position of financial hardship.

- If you need advice about obtaining a sole occupancy order to enable you to stay living at the family home, with your ex-partner required to live elsewhere.

- If you have concerns for your safety or about family violence, and also to obtain advice about protection orders.

- If there is a risk that your ex-partner will sell or transfer property without your knowledge or consent. In this case, you may need to register a caveat on the property.

Urgent access to income & spousal maintenance

If your ex-partner was the main income earner and is denying you access to assets or bank accounts, you should immediately get legal advice.

If you are in a position of financial hardship and have money in a joint bank account, then you should be able to access all or some of those monies to help you get by. The fact that you have taken funds may, however, be considered in the overall property division at a later date. You should be able to justify drawing all of the money and should not do so simply to make life more difficult for your spouse.

A lawyer can assist you initially by negotiating with your ex-partner, in writing, to seek an urgent interim release of money to you or payment to you. If there is no success, then your lawyer can also assist by applying to the Family Law Courts for an interim court order for things such as urgent spousal maintenance.

Sole occupancy

Are you wanting to live in the family home without your ex-partner? Is your ex-partner refusing to leave? If the lease agreement is in joint names or if you both own the property (i.e. both names are on the certificate of title), then the other party will need to agree that you remain in the property. Alternatively, you will need a court order.

I have a client who remained living in the family home after separation and the ex-partner moved out. Her ex-partner then indicated that his intention was to move back into the house around two months later. As you can imagine, from my client's perspective, the thought of having him move back in was awkward and she was not comfortable with the situation. I explained to her that her ex-partner had every legal right to come and go (and live) in the property.

We decided to test the water, so to speak, and she instructed me to write to her ex-partner to put him on notice about her intention to seek sole occupancy and that, ultimately, she wanted the certificate of title transferred to her sole name. Thankfully, my letter was sufficient for the other party to agree not to return. If he had refused to respond to my letter or insisted that he move back into the property, then we would have had to consider an application to the court for sole occupation. I should mention that my client, at that point, had only engaged me for the simple (and inexpensive) task of writing a letter to her ex-partner. I encouraged her to take this approach rather than initiating court proceedings.

 *Can you avoid initiating court proceedings by instructing a lawyer to write a letter on your behalf?*

Intervention orders

The issue around sole occupancy differs again if there is an intervention order in place.

Do you have genuine concerns for your safety? Do you want to remain living in the family home? Perhaps you have children and you do not think that you could afford to relocate. Either way, if you have concerns in relation to your safety, then you should seek police and legal advice in relation to intervention orders. If you have immediate safety concerns, then speak to the police. Most police stations have family violence officers at their stations and they can discuss options with you. They can apply for an intervention order on your behalf if they believe there are genuine concerns for your safety. If the police do not assist you with an intervention order and you do have concerns for your safety, then I urge you to speak with a lawyer at a Legal Aid office or a community legal centre.

The reason an intervention order can be so valuable is that it not only provides you with protection (which is, of course, the first and foremost concern) but also gives you the option of sole occupancy of the property. An intervention order in itself (i.e. without an order of the Family Law Court) can give the protected person the right for sole occupancy. The law has now extended to provide even greater protection to those protected persons who are renting. If you are renting a property in joint names or in your ex-partner's sole name, then the protection of an intervention order may again extend to allow you to remain living at that property.

Do you have genuine concerns for your safety but want to remain living in the family home (whether you own or rent the property and even if it is in your ex-partner's name)? Consider an intervention order rather than applying to the Family Law

Courts. It can sometimes be a much quicker and cost-effective outcome.

Urgent injunction or caveat

We talked about this earlier, but it is worth repeating now we're in the section dealing with property.

Do you have a genuine concern that your ex-partner may sell, dispose of or transfer real estate in their sole name? Is the family home or any investment properties in their sole name? If so, despite you likely having some sort of interest in the property, there is nothing precluding them from selling or transferring the property without your knowledge or consent.

If property is held in joint names (tenants in common or joint tenancy), then your signature will be required on the transfer documents, so you have some protection in that respect. Unfortunately, I have had a number of clients seek legal advice from me too late (after the fact). They just didn't believe there was a genuine risk the other party would dispose of the property. In those matters, the properties have either been transferred or sold. The concern is if the property has been sold at a reduced rate ('mate's rates') or if your ex-partner has disposed of the proceeds of sale. While there are legal ramifications and ways to recoup monies, it can be a costly exercise and is best avoided in the first instance.

A lawyer can assist you to apply for an injunction to prevent your ex-partner from disposing of or selling property. They can also assist to register a caveat to prevent sale or transfer of land that may be in your ex-partner's sole name.

If you have a legal interest in the property, a caveat registered on the certificate of title essentially precludes your ex-partner from being able to transfer the title until you remove the caveat. A caveat is a quick and relatively inexpensive way to protect your interest. You should also get legal advice around obtaining an injunction precluding your ex-partner from further dealing with the property.

Not sure if property is in your ex-partner's name? You can conduct a quick online search with your state's land titles office, which is likely to cost under $30. If the search confirms that property is held in joint names, then you know that you have that protection and are unlikely to need to engage a lawyer to prepare a caveat.

Conduct an urgent online search yourself to check the title of the relevant property. You can also search the name of your ex-partner to see if there are any other properties in which they hold an interest.

Joint monies & bank accounts

Are you concerned that your ex-partner may drain the joint bank account? Is there a risk that they will redraw some or a considerable amount of the mortgage? One immediate step you can take after separation is to contact your financial institution to put in place a 'joint signature' policy, which essentially requires you both to consent to any withdrawal, transfer or redraw of funds. If you have time to do so, then I recommend that you go into your local branch and discuss this with your financial institution.

 *You do not need a lawyer to contact the bank on your behalf to ensure your ex-partner does not redraw your mortgage.*

I have been instructed to write letters to banks for the above purpose, particularly if a matter is urgent. This is, however, something that you can do yourself to save in legal fees.

TIPS – PROPERTY DIVISION – URGENT MATTERS:

- *Before you initiate court proceedings, consider whether a letter from a lawyer could have the desired effect.*
- *If you have genuine concerns for your safety, consider an intervention order.*
- *Conduct an online search to check the title of your property and whether your ex-partner has other properties.*
- *Contact your bank, in person if possible, to request joint signatures be required for any activity related to joint accounts.*

Ways to resolve your property matter

Once you have made some progress by better understanding the factors that are relevant in your property matter, you need to consider **how** you want to progress and formalise your property division.

Negotiate – don't litigate

The options available to resolve your property matter can be summarised as follows:

- Negotiate directly with your ex-partner.

- Negotiate with the use of a family dispute resolution (FDR) service.

- Use a lawyer to assist with the negotiation either by correspondence or lawyer-assisted mediation.

- Opt for a collaborative-law approach, using collaborative lawyers and sometimes other professionals (such as financial advisors and child consultants), to reach an agreement. An agreement is made at the outset to stay out of court.

The goal of any of the above approaches should be to reach an agreement which can then be formalised so as to be legally binding.

If you are able to negotiate directly with your ex-partner, then I would recommend doing so to a certain extent. The more that you can agree in terms of the value of the asset pool and how the overall division may look, the less you will both spend on legal fees.

 *If you are comfortable discussing your property settlement with your ex-partner, then there is benefit to exchanging documents and trying to at least agree on the value of the asset pool prior to having further input from a solicitor.*

FDR services

Family dispute resolution (FDR) services have qualified family dispute resolution practitioners who can assist to mediate your property settlement. These are run through government and community services such as Centacare and Relationships Australia. There are also private mediation services, although they are more costly.

I find that the quality of the FDR depends on the individual practitioner. It is important to keep in mind that the mediators are not lawyers and cannot give legal advice. It is not their role in the FDR process to provide this. I consider FDR a good tool to assist parties to identify the property pool and to negotiate the property agreement. The cost of FDR with a community or government service is nominal and there are likely to be reduced rates if you suffer from financial hardship.

The FDR process is a mediation process whereby each party will attend an individual intake session, with both parties later attending a joint session to discuss the issues. The mediation is relatively informal and any agreement reached will not be legally binding. Most FDR services will recommend that you seek legal advice after the joint session (whether or not an agreement has been reached). The mediator themselves cannot make a decision and does not have any judicial capacity. Sometimes, the mediator will suggest a follow-up joint session, which can also be helpful to advance your negotiation with your ex-partner.

FDR may not be suitable for you if there has been family violence or if there is a power imbalance in the relationship.

If you decide to attempt FDR, then I urge you to read through this book completely beforehand and also, at a minimum, obtain some legal advice.

The discussion that takes place during the FDR session will be confidential and cannot be repeated in court if your matter ever reaches that stage – with the exception of a written and signed agreement. You should, therefore, be wary when signing any document or reaching any final agreement at FDR before you seek legal advice.

Attempt FDR prior to instructing a lawyer to act for you, but do not sign any agreement that has been reached during FDR until you have received legal advice.

I find that using FDR services can work really well when complemented with legal advice. I often refer clients to FDR initially so that they can save fees and try to agree on the asset pool with their ex-partner via mediation rather than having me spend a lot of my time trying to resolve this issue through correspondence. I also find if clients are able to agree on the asset pool with their ex-partner that they are, in fact, more likely to agree on the substantial property settlement. It can do wonders for the negotiation process... in some matters!

You can use FDR as a complementary service and then see a lawyer to assist with and hopefully address more narrowly defined issues. This, in turn, will reduce any legal fees. Unfortunately, many lawyers are unlikely to suggest that you attempt FDR and would prefer to negotiate the entirety of your property settlement using their services.

If you go through the FDR process and do not reach an agreement, then you will typically be issued with an s60I certificate which enables you to initiate proceedings in court. The court will want to see that you have attempted to resolve your matter before allowing your application to the court.

If you know that your ex-partner is not going to engage in the FDR process, then you may still need an s60I certificate. Keep in mind that it is much

> *cheaper to obtain one from a community-based FDR service, though this can take much longer. If you need a certificate urgently, then you can pay more to obtain it from a private service.*

If FDR is not suitable for you for some reason, then you will need to either negotiate with your ex-partner in writing and undergo the discovery process or instruct a lawyer to do this on your behalf. If you are negotiating directly, then try to keep all of your correspondence together so that it can be easily found at a later date if need be. You need a paper trail to show the attempts you have made to exchange documents and negotiate so that, in the event your ex-partner does not engage, you can show the court that you have made these attempts. Remember to try to keep the emotion out of your correspondence and continue to treat this as a business transaction.

If you are putting any offers of settlement to your ex-partner, then mark the correspondence 'without prejudice', meaning that it cannot be reproduced in court at a later date. You want to protect your financial position and if it transpires that you change your mind about an offer or receive advice that it's not a great deal for you, then you will want the opportunity to backtrack. You will find that most lawyers mark their correspondence as 'without prejudice' for this reason.

If you need to engage a lawyer at this point, then give good consideration to what your needs are and what approach is likely to progress your matter. Let's face it, if you are dealing with a narcissist, someone who will not budge from their position or someone who simply has their head in the sand, then how useful will ongoing negotiation be? Is there any point paying a lawyer for ongoing negotiation for, say, six months if you are not getting anywhere?

 ***Don't waste your money on drawn-out negotiation processes when your ex-partner is extremely stubborn, fails to engage or has their head in the sand.***

Informal conferences

Informal conferences are becoming more popular with lawyers, with many of them seeing this as an opportunity to settle matters (or generate legal fees!). My view is that an informal conference can be a really useful tool if you and your ex-partner are open to negotiation and both are keen to resolve your matter without going to court.

Informal conferences generally involve you and your lawyer attending a meeting with your ex-partner and their lawyer. The meeting may take place at one of the legal offices or somewhere neutral. They work best if the issues are narrowed down and there has already been some attempt to exchange and agree at least on the valuation of the asset pool.

If you decide to take this approach, then ask for your fee estimate up front. Can your fees be fixed? Your solicitor may also want a barrister to attend the informal conference. If your matter is not overly complex, then question whether this is absolutely necessary. As soon as you have both a solicitor and barrister attend, your legal fees are likely to double.

 *Fix your fees, if you can, or request an estimate. Check if the attendance of a barrister is entirely necessary if your lawyer wants to invite one.*

Collaborative lawyers

A collaborative approach may be suitable for you if your relationship breakdown has been fairly amicable or if you and your ex-partner are very focused on achieving a peaceful and fair outcome.

The collaborative approach is very much a voluntary process. It involves both of you engaging an independent collaborative lawyer and having number of face-to-face meetings with everybody present. The process focuses on transparency, with a mutual goal to stay out of court. Trained professionals such as financial advisors and child specialists can also be involved during different stages.

 *If you want to explore a collaborative approach, then be sure to speak to someone who is a collaboratively trained practitioner.*

A collaborative approach may be worth exploring if it is important for you to be able to co-parent and maintain a respectful relationship. It can also proceed to a much faster and less expensive outcome than court proceedings. Keep in mind that if there is no agreement reached, you will then be required to obtain another lawyer. The collaborative lawyer assisting you through that process is not able to continue to act for you or to help you if your matter later goes to court.

TIPS – WAYS TO RESOLVE YOUR PROPERTY MATTER:

- *Negotiate – don't litigate. If possible, deal with your ex-partner to negotiate what you can before employing a lawyer.*
- *Attempt FDR but do not sign an agreement without input from a lawyer.*
- *If you require an s60I certificate, it will be cheaper from a community-based FDR service but may take longer to obtain. They can be obtained from a private service if the matter is urgent.*
- *Don't draw out the negotiation process if there's no point and your partner is not likely to budge. This is a waste of money.*
- *If an informal conference is on the cards, ask to fix the fees or for a cost estimate. Question whether the presence of a barrister is necessary.*
- *If you are interested in a collaborative approach, ensure you approach a collaboratively trained practitioner.*

Agreement reached?

HAVE YOU REACHED AN AGREEMENT THROUGH PRIVATE negotiation, with the assistance of a lawyer or via FDR mediation?

It is very important to formalise your agreement. There are various ways to formalise your agreement to ensure it is legally binding and enforceable. These options do not require you to attend court.

The *Family Law Act* (s81) refers to the court having a duty to end financial relations between parties. In effect, this means that both you and your ex-partner should be able to carry on with your lives knowing that neither of you can make a further or future claim against the other. It provides you both with certainty. I have seen married couples separated for over ten years who never got around to applying for a divorce order or formalising their property settlement. You will remember that married couples have twelve months *from the date of the divorce order* to effect their property settlement. If there is no divorce, then this leaves the doors open for either party to start the negotiation process and/or apply for property orders.

Can you imagine receiving correspondence from a lawyer ten years after separation?! Your financial situation changes; generally, we move into a better financial position as our career progresses. Our superannuation increases. The value of our property generally increases. We may have re-partnered and ended up in a much better financial position. We may have now received family inheritances which were not part of the discussion previously. Obviously, those factors affect your financial capacity.

 ***Whichever means were used to reach an agreement for your property settlement, always have the agreement drawn up by a lawyer so that it is legally binding.***

There is interesting case law in relation to lottery winnings, which family lawyers are aware of. It does provide some food for thought. Sure, the chance of winning Tattslotto after separation (or at all!) is low, but can you imagine how you would feel if you did have such a windfall and had to share it with your ex-partner? Ouch. Case law in 2014 saw a wife win the handsome sum of $6 million after separation. It was made clear that assets of the relationship included assets acquired after separation. In that case, there were technical submissions around 'add backs' and 'contribution', which I will not bore you with here. The result, however, was that the husband applied to the court for property division and was found to have an entitlement of $500k of the winnings. The wife not only had to pay this money, but also experienced the stress of Family Law Court proceedings in addition to legal fees. If the property settlement had been formalised prior to the winnings, then it would have been much more difficult for the husband to make a claim.

There are also examples where parties have separated and one party subsequently received a family inheritance. If your property matter has not been formalised, then everything is left open and any future family inheritance will need to be factored into the overall property division. I have spoken to clients who have received family inheritances many years after separation. Having not formalised their property settlement, this means those inheritances are not fully quarantined or protected from their ex-partner.

 *Formalise your property agreement to ensure your ex-partner has no entitlement to any future lottery win, windfall or family inheritance.*

If your agreement involves superannuation splitting, then you will need a lawyer to draft that agreement. Superannuation trustees are very particular in relation to the wording of agreements. They need to be provided with a copy of the draft agreement beforehand to be accorded what is called 'procedural fairness'. They often request changes to the drafting. Once finalised, they will need to be served with a copy of the agreement. It is simply not enough for the member of the trust and the non-member to jointly approach the superannuation trustee with a request to split superannuation. They will not action the splitting request and will tell you that they require either an order of the court, consent minutes of order or a binding financial agreement.

Another reason to formalise your property settlement is in relation to stamp duty. Are you considering transferring the family home from joint names to your sole name? To ensure that you do not pay stamp duty and capital gains tax (CGT) on the transfer, you should have an agreement prepared by a solicitor. Keep in mind that any future sale/transfer may be subject to CGT and you should speak with a financial advisor about this prior to signing an agreement.

 ***Money well spent –** having a lawyer draft your property agreement **to ensure that you do not pay stamp duty on the transfer. The legal fees should be significantly less than calculated stamp duty.***

As lawyers, we have practising certificates enabling us to practise and give legal advice. We also have practising insurance. My point is that if you have come to a lawyer with an agreement that you and your ex-partner have reached, we will naturally want to advise you what your actual entitlement might be or what we see as the pitfalls of the agreement. I personally do not take issue with a client agreeing to any agreement that they want to – it is your entitlement. It is important to me, however, that the decision to proceed is made on an informed basis.

There are two ways to formalise your property agreement after you have reached an agreement via the methods above (i.e. away from court):

1. Consent minutes of order
2. Binding financial agreement

Consent minutes of order

Consent minutes of order for property settlements are complex documents that usually need to be drafted by lawyers. Believe me, I am not just saying that because I am a lawyer! I genuinely believe that this is a complex area of law and if you want to have a crack at drafting consent minutes, then it should only be with respect to parenting matters. I see many clients attempt to DIY property agreements and they are simply requisitioned by the court as they are not in the correct format and the drafting is incorrect.

Consent minutes of order set out the agreement reached between you and your ex-partner. They are signed by you both, along with an application for consent orders which sets out your current financial position. You are required to sign an affidavit at the end of that document as to disclosure and to state that the information you have included in the document is true and correct. Once signed by both parties, they are sent to the court (or lodged online), but you never have to appear in court as there are no actual court hearings. Your lawyer also does not need to attend court, so it certainly is a cheaper option.

A registrar of the court will look over the documents and needs to consider the four-step process and be satisfied that the agreement is fair and equitable. The court will not rubber stamp agreements. If the court is unsure about certain information, then the documents are usually requisitioned or a letter is sent for clarification on certain issues. If they are satisfied that it is a reasonable agreement, then they seal (stamp) the documents so that they have the effect of a binding court order.

You and your ex-partner are able to essentially reach any agreement for property division. It does not need to be an agreement that would be considered equitable by the court. If you do reach an agreement that seems to favour one party over the other or does not fall in line with the four-step process, then in all likelihood the court will not approve the agreement. Do not waste your money instructing a lawyer to draft an agreement if it is unlikely to be approved by the court. Consider the option of a binding financial agreement instead (explained below).

Consent minutes of order are often cheaper to prepare than a binding financial agreement. These agreements do not require a lawyer to give legal advice or sign them. I do recommend you instruct a lawyer to draft them, but the other party is not required to have a second lawyer witness their signature and give them advice. If your communication with your ex-partner is amicable, then you may be able to negotiate sharing the costs of having one lawyer draft the documents. If you decide to take that approach, then you will generally need to make that agreement privately and I do not think it is appropriate for your ex-partner to be making payment into your lawyer's trust account. Also keep in mind that only *one* of you is instructing a lawyer in those circumstances. That lawyer will not give advice to the second party. They will also not meet with them face to face and are unlikely to have any lengthy telephone calls with them. There is an advantage to you instructing the lawyer if you have agreed to share the cost as you will have this benefit.

Reached an agreement? If your ex-partner has a lawyer, can you request that they draft the agreement? This could save you thousands of dollars. If you are both self-represented, can you agree between yourselves to share the cost of paying one lawyer to draft the agreement?

As mentioned, consent minutes of order are sent or filed at the registry without the need to physically attend a court hearing. There is a filing fee, which at the time of writing is $160. Does one of the parties qualify for an exemption for payment of fees? Are you or the other party in receipt of a Centrelink benefit or Health Care Card? If so, then it may be worthwhile arranging for the person with the benefit to file the documents so as to avoid the court filing fee.

Binding financial agreement

A binding financial agreement (BFA) is a document which must be drafted by a lawyer to be legally binding. A BFA can be drawn up at the commencement of a relationship, during a relationship or upon the breakdown of a relationship. BFAs are a newer area of law and we are now starting to see more case law outlining flaws with the agreements and later challenging the validity of the documents – particularly a BFA that is drafted at the commencement of a relationship (a 'prenup').

I generally advise only to consider having a BFA drafted if consent minutes will not be approved by the court.

If the property division is particularly favourable to you and the court is not likely to approve it, then it is probably in your financial interest to have a lawyer draft a BFA. A recent example of this is a client of mine whose ex-husband had moved interstate. He told her that she could have the house and he did not want anything from the property settlement. I was quick to assess this agreement as one which was particularly favourable to my client, and also one that the court was not likely to approve because it did not meet the requirements of the four-step process – it was not likely to be considered fair to the husband. I advised my client to have a BFA drawn up and she and her ex-husband signed that document with independent lawyers. I suspect the advice given to the husband was *not* to sign the agreement; however, parties are ultimately entitled to deal with and divide their property however they see fit.

BFAs set out the agreement in a document that is legally binding *only if* it is drafted properly. A BFA is not registered with the court, nor does it require the approval of the court. In order for a BFA to be valid, it needs to meet a number of criteria, including the following:

- Both parties need to have received independent legal advice (i.e. from different law firms);

- Two independent solicitors have given advice and signed a solicitor certificate at the end of the document;

- Both parties need to make full and frank disclosure about any interest that they have in any assets;

- Neither party can be under duress or undue influence to sign the BFA;

- There must be no unconscionable behaviour by either party;

- The BFA should clearly and accurately report the assets at the breakdown of the relationship and current assets that parties have an interest in; and

- Both parties need to be aware that the BFA essentially acts as a 'bar' to later initiating proceedings for further property division.

BFA drafting should never be a DIY job. I saw a client this year who had drafted his own BFA, with both parties signing it in the presence of a Justice of the Peace. It is not a legally binding document and neither party has protection against future claim or court action.

The practical effect of getting a BFA is that you both need to obtain independent advice. It may still be in your interest to proceed with this option if you are receiving considerably more of the asset pool than you would as assessed under the Act.

Does your agreement see you receiving considerably more of the asset pool than may be considered reasonable by the court? Consider paying for a BFA to be drafted to secure your agreement. Otherwise, if your assets and financial position changes or if you win the lottery or receive a family inheritance, then your ex-partner is likely to be able to pursue further property division.

Time limitations

Beware! There are time limits to seek an order from the court for property division. The general rule is that a married couple has twelve months from the date of divorce and a de facto couple has two years from the date of separation. It is amazing how quickly time can fly by!

 **Ask yourself:** *Could the time limit work in your favour to prevent your ex-partner from claiming property division?*

There may be exceptions if there have been genuine efforts to resolve matters before the expiration of the time limit but, again, each matter is different.

Be mindful of these time limits. If it is in your interest for the time limitation to lapse (i.e. significant assets are in your sole name), that is fine, but if you need to protect your interest in the asset pool, then do not allow it to lapse.

TIPS – PROPERTY AGREEMENT:

- *However you have reached an agreement, you need a lawyer to draft it so that it is legally binding.*
- *To ensure your ex-partner has no entitlement to any future lottery win, windfall or family inheritance, you must formalise your agreement.*
- *Having a lawyer draft your property agreement ensures that you do not pay stamp duty on any transfer of property.*
- *If your ex-partner has a lawyer, request that they draft the binding financial agreement (if one is required). If neither of you has a lawyer, consider sharing the cost for one of you to instruct a lawyer.*

- *Never DIY your BFA draft. You will not end up with a legally binding document.*
- *Be wary of the time limitations, unless letting them lapse is in your favour.*

PART FIVE:
CHILDREN

Parenting matters

As discussed towards the beginning of this book, one of the best things you can do when trying to resolve your parenting matter is to arm yourself with knowledge. The better understanding you have of the principles of Family Law, the more likely you will be able to reach an agreement without the input of a family lawyer.

In 2006, the government set up family relationship centres across Australia to support families to reach an agreement about children. Your local family relationship centre can be a good starting point for general information and referrals.

 *Check out my law firm's online course, which guides you through the Family Law process: www.familylawproject.com.au*

Misconceptions

As with property matters, there are a few misconceptions when it comes to parenting matters. The better you research and understand the legal principles, the more likely you will be to quickly reach an agreement with your ex-partner. Again, we use the legislation and case law as a guide when trying to resolve a parenting matter by agreement outside of court.

The most common misconception that I see is the 50/50 myth. Amendments were made to the *Family Law Act* in 2006 which provide for a presumption of 'equal shared parental responsibility' except in matters where there has been child abuse or family violence. Parental responsibility is in relation to major decisions for the children, such as educational, medical and religious decisions. This is very different from a presumption of *equal shared time* (*shared care*). Unfortunately, this is a really common misconception and one which you are likely to have heard about from a well-meaning friend. The reality is that every family is very different. No two families are the same – each family has their own dynamics and each child has their own unique needs.

There is no presumption that a child will have equal time with their parents after separation. The law says when the court makes an order for shared parental responsibility that it *must* then consider making an order for the children to spend equal time with both parents. But just because the court has to consider this does not mean the order will be made.

When looking at the interests of your child, you may want to start considering everything from your child's point of view. The separation is stressful for you – can you imagine how difficult it is for your child? Your child is also experiencing many changes and it is important to try to keep things as consistent as possible.

Can they remain living in the family home? Can they continue at the same school? Rather than thinking of the time that *you* are entitled to, it can be helpful to try to focus on things from your child's point of view. What relationship are *they* entitled to have with you and your ex-partner? This can sound like a simple concept but I truly believe that trying to switch your mindset can make a profound difference to help you through this difficult time. The changes to the legislation in 2006 were not directed towards parental rights, but rather couched so that *the child* can have a meaningful relationship with both of their parents.

An equal time order can be difficult to achieve, particularly if:

- The children are very young;

- The communication between you and your ex-partner is horrendous (high-conflict matters);

- Your parenting styles completely differ; or

- You live a long distance from each other (and other practical issues).

The social science in this area differs and, of course, many people disagree with certain positions. I suggest that you read the social science in relation to attachment theory. Jennifer McIntosh is a clinical child psychologist and researcher who is generally well regarded by most judges in the jurisdiction. I know a judge who distributes her study as part of an interim court order. You can Google her name and also research other experts around the issue of 'attachment theory in Family Law' to have a better understanding of what the court would consider relevant. Generally speaking, most judges agree with the studies and will show reluctance for shared-care arrangements for very young children.

You may disagree and your matter may be different. You may have a three-year-old who has easily transitioned on a week-about arrangement for the past twelve months. If so, then there may be good grounds to argue that this arrangement should continue. In contrast, you may have a twelve-year-old who has a strong attachment to you and does not want to spend much time with their other parent. Just be aware that if there has never been a shared-care arrangement and you are dealing with very young children, you should not expect that there will be an agreement for equal time.

 **Read up on the social science around children's development and attachment theory.**

The legislation says that children have the right to spend 'substantial and significant time' with their non-residential parent. What does that mean? It does not mean shared care and it does not necessarily mean overnight time. Can you imagine not spending time with your baby or toddler for two weeks? Two weeks for a very little child is a lifetime! Attachments are lost. If you have a very young child, then I suggest not becoming fixated on overnight time but rather the frequency of time. The literature tells us that the years from birth until a child turns four are the years when they are extremely vulnerable and when their attachments are established. The majority of the social science literature focuses on the importance of protecting children at this young and vulnerable age.

Generally speaking, you want to build to overnight time if you are the non-residential parent. It may mean that shared care is the end point that you aim towards, with a gradual increase over time to suit the age of your child and your child's needs. The importance of a very young child having an attachment with their primary carer cannot be understated. Likewise, if you are a child's primary caregiver, you need to understand the importance of facilitating your child frequently spending time with their other parent.

Another respected Family Law judge wrote a paper for a Family Law conference in 2011, whereby she outlined her concern at the number of cases she saw where the parents were seeking orders which seemed inappropriate for the developmental needs of the child.

Ultimately, I suspect a number of you will disagree with what I have outlined above and that is fine. What I do ask, though, is that you take my comments seriously. What I have outlined is generally the position that *the court* would take. Knowing this position will help you in your negotiations and, therefore, help you to be realistic when negotiating the living and time-spending arrangements for your child to try to avoid your matter ending up in court. Conceding that it is not in the best interest of your very young child to spend equal time with each party, or even overnight time with you, does not mean that you are less capable of parenting.

The above information and notion around attachment theory is, of course, invalid if a child is at risk of harm or violence. In those matters, there may be strong arguments for the parent who is placing the child at risk of harm or violence to spend no time with the child.

If you have consulted a lawyer and they have not discussed attachment theory with you, then you should begin that conversation with them and ask how that applies in your family situation. As lawyers, we have an obligation to advise you about what the court is likely to do (or at least the range of orders the court may make). If you are encouraged to pursue a week-about arrangement for a twelve-month-old who has no history of this arrangement, then I would seriously consider getting a second legal opinion.

If you have a lawyer, discuss attachment theory with them if you have not already. Ask questions specific to your matter and about how the social science is likely to apply to your matter. If they have not already discussed this with you, then question why.

When determining the ongoing living arrangements for your children, the types of things to consider are:

- What type of arrangements have been in place post separation?

- How long have those arrangements been in place?

- Who has been the primary carer of the children during the relationship?

- How old are the children? Children in their teenage years should still be guided by an adult decision, but I suspect they will have a view/preference.

- How far apart do you and your ex-partner live?

- How similar are your parenting styles?

Ways to resolve parenting matters without the court

Despite the current differences between you and your partner, if you can reach an agreement outside of court proceedings, then you will almost certainly pave the way to better ongoing communication. Court proceedings are highly stressful and you are encouraged to focus on the negative elements of your ex-partner, as a person and as a parent. Nasty things are said via affidavit material and submissions made during court hearings. It can be costly and that can cause further issues around communication or any chance of co-parenting. Don't get me wrong, some matters require a judicial determination, but if you are focused on trying to resolve your matter without the use of courts, then I recommend that you do.

In fact, the changes to the legislation in 2006 mean that all parties must make a genuine attempt to resolve their parenting matters before applying to the court for an order. Attending family dispute resolution (FDR) is compulsory except in certain situations, such as in matters where there are allegations of family violence or if your matter is urgent.

Family dispute resolution (FDR)

An FDR service can take place through a private service or through a government/community service such as the Family Relationships Centre, Relationships Australia or Centacare. Either you or your ex-partner can initiate the process. Almost all services will first have an individual intake session where you individually attend the service to discuss your current arrangements and the children's needs. Some of these services offer compulsory or non-compulsory seminars beforehand which discuss things such as attachment theory and the best interests of children. There is also a focus on the importance of communication between parents after separation. I have a number of clients who are initially resistant to attending these information sessions; however, they almost always return with positive feedback, saying they found the seminar useful.

If there is an intervention order in place and/or criminal charges, then there is a good chance that the FDR service will not facilitate the mediation. In some circumstances, they will agree to run the mediation via a 'shuttle service', where you are both in separate rooms and the mediator goes between rooms.

Once you have both attended the intake session, you will be invited to attend a joint FDR session with the FDR practitioner (mediator). That practitioner is not able to give either of you legal advice. Each FDR service operates differently, but generally you will find that the joint session may go for up to three hours. The practitioner will work with you both to discuss the needs of your children and see if any agreement can be reached. An option is to reach an interim agreement (parenting plan) on limited issues and then go back for a further mediation session at a later date. This can be a good option if you have only recently separated and the needs of the children are not entirely known. For example, you may trial an arrangement to see how well (or not) the children respond.

I suggest that you obtain some legal advice (even free advice via a Legal Aid service or community legal centre) *prior* to attending the joint FDR session.

The FDR practitioner is not a judicial officer. They cannot make a decision if you and your ex-partner do not agree on parenting arrangements for the children. The practitioner's role is to offer guidance and perhaps make recommendations or give examples as to how your parenting arrangement may look. Ultimately, if there is no agreement, then you will both be issued with a 'Section 60I mediation certificate'.

Please be mindful that anything discussed during the FDR sessions remains confidential, with the exception of any concerns raised in relation to a child's safety (in which case, the FDR practitioner will need to make a mandatory report to Child Protection). This encourages both parties to be open with the communication and discuss various options, which they might not do in a more formal setting (such as court). It is very important to realise that any agreement reached cannot be disclosed to the court at a later date unless the agreement is written and signed by both parties. I suggest that you do not sign any agreement until you have received legal advice.

 *If you do reach an agreement during FDR mediation and you are not sure if the agreement is favourable to you, then do not sign it until you have received legal advice.*

Attendance at FDR is not compulsory. If you are invited to attend, then you do not need to. Likewise, if you initiate the process, you cannot demand that your ex-partner engage in the process. If either of you do not engage or if no agreement is reached, please be aware that an s60I certificate will be issued to the party who arranged the mediation and this is essentially a certificate that then allows that party to initiate court proceedings. If you want to avoid court proceedings, then I suggest that you engage in the process to avoid the other party being issued with an s60I certificate.

There are also private mediation services which are run by qualified FDR practitioners. These private services are generally more expensive than the community-based services run by the Family Relationships Centre and Relationships Australia. Some of the private services offer online options and most of them have a much shorter waitlist, so if time is important to you, it is worth checking what private FDR services are available to you.

Informal conference

If you have a lawyer, then one option may be to attempt to resolve your parenting matter by way of informal conference. This is usually a lawyer-assisted conference which takes place at a lawyer's office. This is likely to be more expensive than using community-based FDR or a private mediation option, but it can be a good option if one party has already engaged a lawyer and you are wanting to avoid court proceedings.

One advantage of an informal conference is that it is likely to be arranged more quickly than community or government-based FDR. However, if cost is a concern for you, I would recommend other options in the first instance before engaging a lawyer for an informal conference.

Legal Aid Family Law conference

The Legal Aid offices in each state facilitate Family Law conferences, which are also lawyer assisted. They take place at the local Legal Aid office. The conferences usually have a very high success rate, as each party has a lawyer assisting them and the mediators usually have a background of having worked as a family lawyer (although their role is not to provide legal advice). Only one party needs to qualify for a grant of legal aid for this conference. I have attended many of these conferences and certainly recommend them. Not only are you receiving legal advice but you can also remain in control – the mediator is not a judicial officer and cannot make any decision for you. No decision is enforced on you.

 *Some people will not qualify for a grant of legal aid with the exception of some limited funding for a Legal Aid lawyer-assisted conference. If you are on a low income, then it is worthwhile seeing if you qualify for this funding.*

Lawyer-assisted negotiation

Lawyer-assisted negotiation is essentially where you instruct a lawyer to write to your ex-partner (or their lawyer) to negotiate parenting agreements.

Engaging a lawyer when a parenting matter is urgent can be a very effective way to put your ex-partner on notice about your concerns and also put them on notice that if certain actions are or are not taken, you will initiate court proceedings (if relevant). This can be quite an effective way to deal with an urgent or interim matter without actually having to apply to the court. Sending a letter from a lawyer can certainly prompt a response.

The appropriateness of ongoing negotiation really depends on your particular matter and the complexities. If there has been family violence and you do not want to participate in FDR (or the FDR service will not accept you for that reason), then it may be a good idea to try to negotiate parenting arrangements through a lawyer rather than immediately opting for initiating court proceedings. Proposals for living and time-spending arrangements can be put to your ex-partner by letter.

 *Only use lawyer-assisted negotiation if it is the best option for you. It may otherwise be a waste of money.*

Things you can do to encourage an agreement

If you are trying to resolve your matter directly with your ex-partner or through one of the other methods discussed above, then it may not be uncommon for your ex-partner to raise concerns about your parenting skills. While you may not agree with their concerns, you need to start thinking about how you can resolve your matter without proceeding to court. Weigh up whether other things can be done to appease your ex-partner's concerns. Can you put things in place to offer them reassurance? This will be quicker and less stressful than court proceedings.

An example of this is where, for whatever reason, you have not spent time with your child for a considerable time. Now, it may not be your fault that you have not been able to spend time with your child. In fact, it may even be your ex-partner's doing! Putting aside any frustration that you may feel around the issue, it would be worthwhile considering having supervised time with your child with a private supervised service or a children's contact service to keep the negotiations moving. Otherwise you may be left in a position of stalemate and not be able to spend any time with your child.

If you initiate court proceedings (which can be an incredibly slow process), then the judicial officer might be of the view that some sort of supervised time should take place. This does not concede that your child is at risk, but recognises that the relationship needs to be rebuilt or your ex-partner needs to be appeased to reach your end goal. If money is not a concern to you and your ex-partner has unrealistic expectations, then you may need to initiate court proceedings as soon as possible to secure some time with your child.

 *Remember your end goal and think of ways that you can achieve what you want without the ongoing expense of lawyers and court.*

Other things that you may want to consider are doing parenting courses and courses such as Circle of Security and Kids Are First. Both of those courses are well regarded by the court and if you ever end up in court, then it would be helpful to have already completed them. Taking the initiative to participate in these types of courses can also assist during the negotiation. If your ex-partner has concerns about your communication or parenting skills, then completing these courses goes a long way to support your commitment to properly care for your child. You could even propose that your ex-partner complete the same courses.

Have there been allegations of violence or allegations around your anger management? Has there been an intervention order or criminal charges against you? Anger management courses can be helpful and can also assist to persuade your ex-partner that you are taking all necessary steps. Most courses recommended through services such as the Family Relationships Centre and Relationships Australia receive good feedback, even from reluctant clients!

However, be careful in relation to taking anger management courses and obtain legal advice before doing so. You don't want it to look like an admission that you have anger management issues.

Are there any parenting or communication courses that you can complete? Even if you think you don't need to do them, they can be good to have on your belt to use to your advantage in negotiation. My clients who complete these courses somewhat reluctantly usually report back positively!

One of the common allegations I see made after separation and during the negotiation process is that one party is a drug user. You can easily satisfy your ex-partner that you are not using illicit drugs by undergoing a hair follicle test. These days, I am seeing companies setting up testing services which are more affordable but still comply with Australian protocol. You can now have a hair follicle test done for under $500, which will usually show your drug and alcohol use for the preceding three months. If you're not using illicit drugs, then that is a quick way to nip such allegations in the bud. Pardon the pun. Speaking of marijuana, did you know that marijuana can remain in your system for a very long time, depending on the frequency and duration of use? I have clients who undergo random drug-screen tests who may not have smoked for a couple of weeks, but the results still show.

If you cannot afford a hair follicle test, then you may want to agree to be subjected to a couple of random drug-screen tests. They need to be done on a random basis to adequately satisfy the other party. If they are not random, then a drug user will simply avoid using drugs such as ICE in the days prior to the testing. Most random drug-screen tests compliant to standard (the court required standard is AS/NZ4308:2008) will cost around $150. If you are not using drugs, then this may be an economical way to stop the allegations made by your ex-partner. If your matter ultimately does go to court, then the fact you willingly participated in drug tests will be viewed favourably. You cannot really lose... unless you're actually using illicit drugs!

If you are using illicit drugs, please turn your mind to obtaining professional help. I have added resources at the end of this book to help you if you would like to reduce or cease illicit drug and alcohol use.

If you have concerns about your ex-partner using drugs, consider offering to pay for their test so that you have some peace of mind.

Not using drugs? It may be worthwhile obtaining a hair follicle test or submitting to a couple of random drug-screen tests to avoid court proceedings and progress things more quickly.

As an aside, if you are using marijuana occasionally, then my experience is that the court does not take too dim a view on this if you are not using while the children are in your care. If you suspect that your matter will end up in court, then my advice is to try to at least reduce your marijuana use, which you can do through a number of free drug and alcohol support services.

TIPS – PARENTING MATTERS:

- Read up on the social science around children's development and attachment theory.
- If you have a lawyer, discuss attachment theory with them.
- If you're not sure it's favourable to you, do not sign an agreement reached in FDR mediation without obtaining legal advice.
- Is it worthwhile seeing if you qualify for funding for a Legal Aid lawyer-assisted conference?
- Only use lawyer-assisted negotiation if it is the best option for you. Don't waste your money.
- Keep in mind that court comes with the expense of ongoing proceedings and lawyers. Remember your end goal and try to achieve it in other ways.
- Consider completing parenting or communication courses to use to your advantage during negotiation.
- If you're not using drugs, submit to a hair follicle test or random drug-screen tests to make progress and be viewed favourably by the court if things reach that stage.

24

Formalising parenting matters

IF YOU REACH A WRITTEN AGREEMENT VIA MEDIATION OR conference, then in all likelihood it will be a parenting plan. Likewise, you may have reached a written agreement with your ex-partner about the living arrangements of the children and also had this drawn up to constitute a parenting plan. It is not uncommon for parties to have reached an agreement with respect to parenting matters but still have outstanding property matters (or vice versa).

One of the concerns that you are likely to research or be advised about is that a parenting plan is not in itself a legally binding document. You may be advised to formalise the parenting plan into a court order via consent minutes of order (in a similar way to that discussed in the previous part of the book in relation to property settlements). I do not necessarily agree. Generally speaking, if you are relatively confident that your ex-partner will comply with the terms of a parenting plan, then I suggest saving your money. In saying that, ensure that the parenting plan is written and signed in case your ex-partner decides that they are no longer going to comply. You will then be able to annex it to an affidavit if you need to initiate court proceedings at a later date to seek formal orders.

You can pay a lawyer to draft consent minutes to formalise your parenting plan, but think about the purpose of doing this. If there is poor communication between you and your ex and you are concerned that they will not comply with a parenting plan, this may be a good reason to formalise the agreement, but if your ex-partner decides not to comply with the binding court order or withholds your child, then you are still likely in the same position of having to apply to the court for enforcement of those orders. A court order that is not being complied with will need to be re-visited by the court for enforcement. You cannot simply take your court order to the police or another authority and automatically have your ex-partner made to comply. Any urgent matter where you are seeking the recovery of children or have new concerns for child protection will require fresh court proceedings, even if you have a court order. Even if you have parenting orders in place, the state police and the Australian Federal Police cannot action a location or recovery order without a new order of the court.

If you have a written parenting plan, then you can equally initiate urgent proceedings for enforcement if, for example, your ex-partner has withheld the children. In any event, if the breach is minor then you are unlikely to want to take it to court.

In saying that, most people will take court orders more seriously and are more likely to comply with them than a parenting plan.

Depending on your level of communication and trust with your ex-partner, you may not need your parenting plan formalised by way of a court order. This tip could save you thousands of dollars!

There are, however, times when it is actually recommended that you pay a lawyer to have a parenting plan converted to consent minutes of order so as to have a binding court order. An example of this may be when you have reached an agreement which is particularly favourable to you and you want to ensure that it remains in place. There is case law (*Rice & Asplund*) which stipulates that unless there has been a significant change to your circumstances, the parties cannot keep taking a matter back to court to change orders. If you have orders in place that are favourable to you, then it will make it difficult for your ex-partner to later change their mind and/or apply to the court to vary the agreement.

Does your ex-partner have a lawyer? If so, ask that they prepare the legal agreement. This can save you thousands of dollars. If neither of you have a lawyer, discuss jointly sharing the cost of having a lawyer draft the agreement.

No agreement

Okay. So you have been unable to reach an agreement directly with your ex-partner or via any of the above methods. Or perhaps your ex-partner is simply not engaging or has their head in the sand. It may be that you have no option but to initiate court proceedings. If you do, then ensure that you understand what is involved prior to initiating. If you do seek the assistance of a lawyer, then go back to the first chapters in this book to ensure that you are choosing wisely and preferably on a fixed-fee basis.

If you have made a genuine attempt to resolve your matter, then you may have no option but to initiate court proceedings. Other examples where you may need to initiate proceedings include:

- Where there is a risk to the child and you need to ensure your child's protection;

- Matters where there has been family violence and you do not feel safe or comfortable using an alternative method of dispute resolution;

- An urgent recovery application – where your ex-partner has removed your child from your care and you are seeking their return;

- Where your ex-partner is withholding your child from you and refuses to facilitate contact;

- A location order if you are unsure of the whereabouts of your child – you can apply to the court for an order from the Department of Education or Centrelink, for example, to release the address that they have on file for your ex-partner.

An order is not always needed

Sometimes, the best option in your situation may be to do nothing. If no agreement is reached via the options discussed in this book, it does not necessarily mean that the next appropriate step for you is to initiate court proceedings. The reality is that if the children are in your care and they are safe or if your ex-partner has stopped spending time with the children, then you may not need to do anything. It may be in your interest to wait and see what, if anything, your ex-partner does.

It is quite common for me to speak to a client who says to me, '*I want to apply to court for full custody.*' When we delve into the practical reality of their situation, it transpires that the children are already in their full-time care and their ex-partner is not even spending time with the children. It would not be sensible in that situation to initiate court proceedings. It is very rare for the court to simply make an order for full-time 'custody' without hearing from the other party in relation to the orders that they are seeking. If you were to initiate the proceedings, then you would essentially be inviting your ex-partner to a process where they are invited to file responding documents setting out the orders they are seeking.

In most cases, your ex-partner needs to be served with your application and be invited to participate in the proceedings. You may even fall in a position where the children are spending more time with your ex-partner because you initiated the court proceedings.

Family violence & children

It would be remiss of me to write about parenting matters and not address the issue of family violence. The *Family Law Act* was amended in July 2012, resulting in the Act having a more definitive definition of family and domestic violence and even providing examples of what constitutes 'violence' under the Act.

The law is very clear that you do not need to experience physical violence to be a victim of family violence. Verbal and psychological abuse and simply being fearful of your partner or ex-partner may constitute family violence.

If you are currently experiencing family violence or were in a relationship of domestic violence, then it is very important to speak to a lawyer as soon as possible. I know that this book recommends many money-saving tips and 'lawyer-avoidance' tips; however, there are many family violence legal services available where you can receive free legal advice. You can also receive free legal advice from a Legal Aid office or community legal centre in the first instance.

You should receive the legal advice before attempting negotiations with your ex-partner in any form. It may be that you are advised not to facilitate or allow your ex-partner to spend any time with the children due to concerns for their welfare. One of the aims of the Act is to ensure that children are protected from physical and psychological abuse. This includes where a child has been exposed to abuse (i.e. they have witnessed family violence). The definition of family violence extends to psychological harm, where one party has been threatening, coercive or controlling of the other party. You also should not feel as though you need to personally facilitate or supervise any time.

Intervention orders

I have discussed in this book the benefit of an intervention order in terms of right of occupancy or sole occupancy of a house owned or rented by you or your ex-partner. The protection extends as far as allowing the protected person to reside in the family home even if it is a rental property in your ex-partner's name. If you skimmed or skipped the property section but you have concerns for your safety, then I recommend going back and reading that section.

If an intervention order is in place, it is not uncommon for it to have been made at around the time of separation. It is not uncommon for there to be a situational event that may cause one party to apply for an intervention order for their protection.

If you have been served with an intervention order, then this is a time when you should *seek legal advice*. Being named on an order, even if it includes your children, does not mean that you cannot spend time with your children. This is another common misconception. It may be that you will need to initiate court proceedings to seek an order to spend time with your children, but it is not something you should put off purely on the basis of there being an intervention order in place. Unfortunately, I often see people (usually men) putting off getting legal advice or pursuing time with their children because they mistakenly think that an intervention order precludes them from doing so.

If you are listed as a protected person on an intervention order and if your children are also listed as protected persons, then you may want to put a hold on everything. In those circumstances, there is often no legal requirement for you to facilitate time between your ex-partner and your children. If the intervention order extends to protect the children, then you also have the protection of knowing that your ex-partner cannot approach them or collect them from school. You will need to consider whether it is worthwhile doing anything at all. If you are applying for legal aid for court proceedings, then you may not qualify because Legal Aid will determine that the children are with you and that they are safe and there is no need for a court order. If your ex-partner has initiated Family Law Court proceedings, then that changes the situation and you will likely qualify for funding (presuming you meet their other guidelines).

An intervention order may give you the protection that you and your children need. This is another reason to avoid court.

I have some clients who seem surprised when I explain to them that the intervention order is really all they need for their protection and I actually discourage them from initiating court proceedings.

Some clients want to ensure that the other party does not initiate court proceedings. In those circumstances, we think outside the box and perhaps look at a Family Law mediation on a private basis or through Legal Aid as a tactic to deter the other party from initiating proceedings. It can also be reassuring for some clients to do *something*, as they may be scared that simply withholding the children will piss off their ex-partner. I can almost guarantee it will! This is one complex area that would benefit from some legal input based on your particular circumstances.

TIPS – FORMALISING PARENTING MATTERS:

- *Don't assume that you need your parenting plan formalised by way of a court order. If there's no serious need to, then you could save thousands of dollars.*
- *If you are formalising an agreement and your ex-partner has a lawyer, ask that they prepare the legal agreement. If neither of you have a lawyer, consider sharing the fees of having a lawyer draft the agreement.*
- *An intervention order may give you and your children the protection you need, meaning you can avoid court.*

Child support

Child support is another area of Family Law which is dealt with independently of parenting arrangements, property settlements and divorce applications. Property settlements do not usually factor in what child support is (or isn't) being paid.

Child support is the amount payable to one parent to provide financial support to children of the relationship. The amount of child support payable, if any, will clearly be dependent on any living arrangements that you have in place for the children; however, you do not need to wait to formalise parenting agreements prior to commencing the child support process. The amount payable also takes into account the financial position of both parents.

A good place to start for general information is the Services Australia website (previously and commonly known as the Child Support Agency website). The website includes up-to-date care percentages and tells you the number of nights per year children need to be in a parent's respective care to effect those payment amounts.

 **Spend some time looking at the Services Australia (Child Support Agency) website: csa.gov.au**

The formal calculation and amount of child support payable will differ for every family. The calculation can be quite complex; however, the calculators on the website can be a good starting point.

Parents do not need to have their child support arrangements registered with or assessed by the Child Support Agency. But if an arrangement is assessed by and registered with the Agency, then there are options for the Agency to collect payments or for the parents to make arrangements for private payment of the assessed amount. Some parents will make private arrangements with payment amounts differing from the amount that the government assesses as payable. There are options for various agreements to be registered with the Agency.

 **Always ascertain what the assessed amount via the Agency is (i.e. what your entitlement would be or what the payable amount would be) before reaching a private agreement with the other parent.**

Most Legal Aid offices across Australia have a section of expert child-support lawyers who provide advice solely on child support. In my experience, they are very knowledgeable, particularly since they specialise in the area. They offer free advice, which is not means tested, so regardless of your income and assets, you are likely to qualify for some legal advice about child support. They also may be able to help you with any court application with respect to child support. The Legal Aid child-support lawyers are independent of Services Australia (the Child Support Agency) meaning that anything you discuss with them is confidential and not relayed back or reported to the Agency. I frequently refer my current clients to the Legal Aid child-support lawyers to get free advice about child support matters as a way of minimising my clients' legal fees.

 *Even if you have a lawyer for your parenting or property matter, seek separate free legal advice from the child support section of your state Legal Aid office.*

The formal care arrangements that you have in place may affect how much child support you are assessed as having to pay or receive. If important to you, you should factor in the child support care percentages (number of nights per fortnight the children are with each of you) prior to formalising any parenting plan or parenting order.

 *Are the care arrangements for your children going to affect the amount of child support you will receive or pay? Know the figures prior to formalising your parenting matter.*

As mentioned earlier, there is nothing precluding you and the other parent from reaching any agreement with respect to child support payments. You do not need to fall in line with the assessed amount of the Agency. If you do reach an agreement which is favourable to you, then you may want to consider speaking with a lawyer to have that agreement formalised so that it remains binding. You will need to make a cost assessment when it comes to the cost of a lawyer formalising that agreement for you.

TIPS – CHILD SUPPORT:

- *Visit the Services Australia (Child Support Agency) website: csa.gov.au*
- *Look up your entitlement/amount payable according to Services Australia before reaching a private agreement with the other parent.*
- *Seek free legal advice from the child support section of your state Legal Aid office (even if you have a lawyer!).*
- *Be aware that care arrangements may affect the amount of child support.*

PART SIX:
COURT

26

Initiating court proceedings

I SINCERELY HOPE THAT YOU ARE ABLE TO RESOLVE YOUR Family Law matter without going to court. None of my clients has ever walked out of the court building with me, saying, *'Gee, that was a fun experience!'* The process can take years and can be financially draining.

Remember that there is always an option for you to take a pragmatic approach to your negotiations and to make commercial decisions to resolve your parenting and property settlements at any stage. Is it worth incurring legal fees or the stress and time away from work if you have to use the court system on a self-represented basis? Are there any other ways that you can avoid the court system?

I do understand that sometimes there is no other option. If, for whatever reason, you *have* ended up in our Family Law Court system as an applicant or respondent, then ensure you have a good team behind you.

Initiating procedure

If you decide that you want to initiate proceedings yourself (or if you are advised to do so by a lawyer), then be mindful that the Family Law rules require you to *genuinely attempt* to resolve the dispute before doing so. A genuine attempt may include negotiation and attending FDR.

There are exemptions where a property matter is urgent or if there are interim orders sought which are urgent, if there are allegations of fraud, if the other party is not engaging in the process and/or refusing to negotiate, or if there has been family violence. There are also other technical legal exceptions, such as a time limitation nearly expiring or other legal grounds. As a general rule, if your matter does not fall within the above exceptions, then you must show a genuine attempt to first negotiate.

A component of pre-action procedure is the duty to make full and frank disclosure of all relevant material and facts. Be mindful of this duty, otherwise you do run the risk of a cost order being made against you.

The purpose of pre-action procedure is to ensure that the parties are not put to unnecessary or additional legal expense.

 *Avoid a cost application against you by ensuring that you have complied with pre-action procedure.*

Only go to court if it is unavoidable

As lawyers, we have a duty to advise you that there are ways to resolve a dispute aside from initiating court proceedings. We are also required to advise you around your duty of disclosure and pre-action procedure. If any lawyer does not advise you of these obligations but instead encourages you to initiate court proceedings straight away... please beware!

The reality is that sometimes court proceedings are necessary and will, in fact, be a quicker and cheaper way for you to resolve your matter. At other times, you will be served with documents and named a respondent and have your hand forced into proceedings.

There are currently changes underway, with a merger between the Federal Circuit Court and the Family Court of Australia coming into place from late 2021. The intention of the court merger is to resolve many of the difficulties with the system, including bringing about a single set of rules and a single entry point for all Family Law matters. The intention is to reduce delays and the chronic backlog of matters; however, I can tell you from experience that a change in the structure of the courts alone will not be sufficient.

Families who rely on the court to help them resolve matters at the end of a relationship have a right to a system which is easy to navigate, and provided at the lowest possible price. That is not the current experience of the court system. The Law Council of Australia expressed numerous concerns about the court merger prior to the merger approval and has said, 'There is no doubt that Family Law is factually and legally complex, emotionally-charged and produces life altering consequences for families and children.' This is why families deserve better. As things stand at the moment, I cannot recommend a client enter the court system unless entirely necessary.

 *Avoid going to court if at all possible.*

Going to court

The breakdown of a relationship can be a time of enormous financial and emotional stress for families. If you are required to navigate the Family Court system, then this is likely to cause even greater financial stress.

The Family Court system experiences long delays, drawn-out cases and can be expensive in terms of legal costs. You will also be in a position where a group of strangers are about to enter your life. It can be a particularly stressful time, so ensure you have all of your legal and non-legal supports in place.

It is no secret that the Family Law Court system is overwhelmed and slow. The delays in the system are unacceptable for families and no doubt put enormous pressure on our judges. The changes in the law in 2006 requiring parties to mediate before using the court system do not appear to have reduced the wait times and backlog of matters. The courts are dealing with many complex matters, particularly parenting matters and matters where there are allegations of family violence, mental illness and child abuse.

The reality is that the majority of matters in the court system will settle by agreement without the need to go to trial. Interestingly, many matters will settle at the time a matter is listed for trial, once trial dates and filing deadlines are given. This can place further emotional and financial pressure on parties to reach an agreement to avoid either running a trial on a self-represented basis (what a nightmare!) or having to pay barristers to run the trial (which is where the big bucks can kick in).

This chapter provides tips for navigating the system and saving money while doing so.

Which court?

This was previously a common question; the entry point for Family Law matters was either the Federal Circuit Court or the Family Court of Australia. Up until late 2021, the Federal Circuit Court handled approximately ninety per cent of Family Law matters, with the Family Court acting as a specialist jurisdiction for more complex matters. At the time of writing, the intention is that there will be one court with one single entry point and a consistent set of rules.

Tips we've met so far that are relevant to court

It may be that you've skipped straight to this section. Or you may have read sections previously while you were not in the court system but have now unfortunately found yourself in court. If you are in court, I recommend that you go back and read the following sections in *Chapter 4: Taking back control*, which are applicable to you whether your court proceedings are in relation to property or parenting matters:

- 'Arm yourself with knowledge' – page 31

- 'Wear your business hat' – page 35

- 'Understand grief and loss' – page 38

- 'Understand that nobody is a winner' (this is *particularly* important in the court system!) – page 41

If you are thinking of engaging a lawyer, then read the chapters in Part Two – these will help you choose a lawyer and also help you save money when it comes to legal fees.

If you have parenting matters, then I recommend that you read Part Five of the book. The chapters will give you a better understanding of the social science around parenting arrangements and the common misconceptions in parenting matters. It is particularly important that you arm yourself with this knowledge now that you are in a court environment.

Earlier in the book, I discuss completing parenting courses, anger management courses and drug testing and how you can be proactive in taking steps to address these things in parenting disputes. Now that you are in court, it may be even more important to be proactive and do everything possible to best position yourself with the court. As I mention, it is frequently ordered by the court that parties complete certain courses. If you are able to do these things before they are court ordered, being proactive and predicting what orders may be made by the court may help you to better position yourself. Rather than having your matter adjourned and delayed waiting for those things to be done, completing them as soon as possible may mean there are fewer delays in your proceedings.

If your court proceedings are in relation to property division, then I recommend you read Part Three of the book. It is really important to have a good understanding of the four-step process and the relevant sections of the *Family Law Act* to better understand how the court will determine your property matter. You will want a good understanding of the asset pool and how to value property and you will want to understand the 'discovery' process – these tips are all covered in this part of the book.

Consider further legal advice

Now that your matter is in court, consider obtaining further legal advice, and obtain procedural information in relation to the court process. You will find that things are quite different now that you are in the court system and not negotiating directly with your ex-partner or using mediation. If you cannot afford a lawyer, then remember my tips in Part Two in relation to free legal advice and unbundled legal options, such as obtaining one-off legal advice.

Many Legal Aid services are a good starting point to obtain procedural information in terms of what to expect in court.

Obtaining procedural information will help you to know what documents need to be filed and what to expect in various types of court hearings.

 *Even if you have received previous legal advice, now that your matter is in court it is pertinent to obtain some updated legal and procedural advice about what to expect during the court process.*

Reassess whether you qualify for legal aid

You may have previously sought some legal aid funding but been rejected, for various reasons, on merit. Now that your matter is in court, will you qualify for legal aid funding? Is it worth making the enquiry?

If there have been allegations of family violence in your matter and it is being listed for trial, then you may qualify for free government funding for property and parenting matters which is *not* means or merit tested. In other words, it does not matter how much you earn or what your asset pool is. If there have been allegations of family violence in your matter, then I strongly recommend you read the section 'Family Violence & Cross-Examination Scheme' in Chapter 6 to ascertain if you qualify (page 61).

Now that your matter is in court, you may qualify for legal aid funding even if your application was previously rejected on the grounds of merit.

Small property pools

If you are considering initiating proceedings for your property division, then first ascertain if your property pool is less than $500,000. If so, be aware that a number of registrars around Australia have a dedicated list to resolve small property pools in a more cost-effective manner. The names may change, but currently the 'PPP500' list is a specialised small property pool list which simplifies the process, and the forms are generally less difficult to complete. More registrars have been allocated to assist judges to deal with the backlog and case management to try to resolve these small property matters more efficiently.

Matters in these small property pools will still require document exchange and disclosure. In all likelihood, you will be referred to a conciliation conference. The focus, however, will be to ensure the process is less difficult to enable more people easier access. Any agreement reached or orders made by the court will still provide you with the standard protection and entitlements.

Check if your registry has a specialist property pool list for matters less than $500k. This is particularly useful for really small asset pools, enabling you to navigate the process yourself rather than pay tens of thousands of dollars towards legal fees.

Spend time in court

I recommend that all of my clients spend some time in court, preferably *before* their matter is heard. The Family Law Courts are generally 'open' courts, meaning that the public can sit in on most hearings. Most matters stay in the same 'docket' of the same judge, who will have conduct of your matter from start to finish. All judges have different styles and expectations and it can, therefore, be particularly helpful to sit in on the duty list of your judge to get a feel for what to expect. I recommend this to all clients, even those who have a lawyer representing them in court. It can also assist to help you feel more comfortable with the process and give you a better idea of what to expect.

 **Spend time observing the court list of the judge that your matter is listed before.**

Bad conduct & costs

Now that you are in the court system, it's important to have a grasp of some of the dirty tricks that may be used by your ex-partner or their lawyer. It is also important to understand how 'costs' are dealt with by the court, as it is quite different from other court systems.

In the first instance, it is important to be aware that the *Family Law Act* outlines the general concept in Family Law matters that each party pays their own legal costs.

There are exceptions where the court can make a cost order against one party. The court will consider issues such as the conduct of the parties during the proceedings and their compliance (or non-compliance) with orders. Circumstances where a party may claim costs include: where the proceedings were necessary due to the other party failing to comply with orders; in the case of vexatious and unnecessary applications; and where the other party fails to engage in negotiations.

The reality is that we see discretionary cost orders awarded as the exception rather than the rule. The other thing to keep in mind is that it is quite common for an application for costs to be deferred until after trial, even though the bad behaviour of one party often takes place early in the proceedings. The other factor the court has to consider when making a cost order against one party is their actual capacity to pay. If your ex-partner is unemployed and/or in receipt of a grant of legal aid, then it may be even more difficult to achieve a cost order in your favour.

While it may be worthwhile seeking a cost order in your matter, keep in mind it is discretionary and certainly not guaranteed. Cost orders will also be subject to scale and will not necessarily cover the actual legal fees you have incurred.

Burning off
The concept of 'burning off' is where the other party tries to burn through your legal budget by pressing each and every conceivable point (contesting all issues) and making numerous applications. Unfortunately, I have seen this practice encouraged by some lawyers.

Ex-partners who come out with statements like *'I'll make sure you end up with nothing'* are more likely to use this tactic.

This naturally puts the person in the weaker financial position at a disadvantage, as they are likely left having to respond to each of these issues. If you are paying a lawyer, then you will be required to pay them for all of the ongoing advice and representation they provide in relation to this. If you are self-represented, then it may cause financial strain because it takes up more of your time and you have to take further leave from employment. Regardless of whether you are instructing a lawyer or are self-represented, it is certainly likely to take an emotional toll.

 *Your ex-partner may be using money or persistence essentially as a weapon to drag out the case, hoping that you will give up. Once you are aware of this, you are likely to be able to put supports in place to help you deal with the issue and also consider seeking cost orders in your favour, if appropriate.*

Hearing by ambush

Another dirty trick we see is commonly known as 'hearing by ambush'. This typically occurs when one party files and serves affidavits and documents at the last minute, just prior to a hearing. In some circumstances, the judges will not allow documents that have not been served at least two business days (or at another court-ordered time) prior to the hearing. At other times, the court may consider the content of the material critical to consider, particularly in parenting proceedings if the material is relevant to the welfare of children.

One of the difficulties with hearing by ambush is that you have often waited months for a hearing date and the last thing you want to do is have a hearing adjourned and put off to another date to give you the opportunity to formally respond. When you are served at the last minute, it really can make it difficult to adequately prepare and respond in time.

Be aware of 'hearing by ambush' and be as prepared as possible prior to each and every hearing to deal with any new or last-minute matters that may be raised by your ex-partner. If possible, well before the hearing date, turn your mind to pre-empting the types of last-minute issues that may be raised and have your supporting information and evidence ready in advance.

False allegations

I hear of this time and time again when I speak with clients who say they have been falsely accused of terrible things such as family violence, child abuse and drug use so their ex-partner can gain legal leverage. The nature of the Family Law Court system is that the parties are required to file affidavit material, which is a sworn statement setting out your version of events and concerns. Often, early in the proceedings, the only information that judges will have is the two versions of affidavits or a 'he said, she said' scenario. The difficulty for the judge is that they do not know where the truth lies and in those early days in the proceedings (interim hearings), it is simply not possible to test the evidence to make a finding.

False allegations are less likely to hold weight in the long term, once the evidence has been tested... but you need to be able to get to that point!

I have seen firsthand the impact that false allegations have had on the mental health of clients. Court is already stressful enough; dealing with false allegations against you and feeling as though you have to prove your innocence or rebut the allegations can be deeply disturbing.

If you are the subject of false allegations, then I cannot stress enough the importance of leaning on your mental health support services. In terms of a legal perspective, remember that the court is assisted to obtain independent information to make findings or to deal with allegations and concerns raised in affidavits. The court is likely to take a cautious approach in the first instance, but this does not mean that you should back down and not position yourself as best as possible. I have detailed below the types of independent information used by the court to assist the judge to make decisions.

Subpoena & s69ZW

A subpoena is a summons issued to either a person, a government department or a private business. In Family Law proceedings, we usually see a subpoena directed to departments such as Child Protection, the state police and state education departments. In property proceedings, you may need to issue a subpoena to places such as financial institutions if you do not think your ex-partner has been transparent in disclosing their financial position.

Before issuing a subpoena, consider whether the information is relevant and if it is likely to assist you. Objections to a subpoena can be made on a number of grounds, including if someone is seen to be simply on a 'fishing expedition'. Also consider whether there is likely to be any information that is potentially incriminating for you.

A subpoena is filed with the court and then served on the relevant person or department with a timeframe to provide documents to the court registry. The judge will not look at that bundle of documents; it is for the parties to view and copy as appropriate and put to the court formally.

If you have a lawyer and they have issued a subpoena in your matter, can you attend court yourself to view and copy all of the material to reduce your legal fees?

Another way to have the same information presented to the court from Child Protection, the state police or the education department of your state is through what is called a s69ZW order. This is an order made by the court which is directed to various government agencies. The court makes these orders frequently as a way of obtaining relevant information – usually in parenting matters. Again, the relevant department produces the material to the court registry and the parties and legal representatives (subject to an order or permission) can view and copy material.

When the court makes these orders, you are not required to draft or file any documents or serve anything on the government department or service provider. There is also no filing fee, which you would normally pay the court when you file a subpoena. It is, therefore, a good option to consider. Ask your lawyer about this if you have a lawyer, as it is likely to save you legal fees compared to your lawyer issuing a subpoena. If you are self-represented, then you may ask the court to make a s69ZW order or seek that order in your documents, if appropriate.

 *Ask yourself: Is a s69ZW order more appropriate than a subpoena to help you obtain relevant information?*

Family consultants – s11F meetings

Familiarise yourself with what is involved when you meet with a family consultant. Sometimes, the court will order an 's11F' meeting, which may or may not involve the children. Spend time familiarising yourself with the process well before any meetings so that you are as well prepared as possible. As a general rule, you should also ensure your documents are filed well in advance of any meeting to ensure the family consultant has read them.

Family reports

As with the meetings with the family consultant, it is also important that you arm yourself with knowledge in relation to what is involved in the family report process. The court frequently makes orders for parties to attend a meeting with a family consultant or a private practitioner to prepare a detailed report with recommendations for the court. To best place yourself in proceedings, ensure that you understand what is involved in the process. The judge is not bound to follow any recommendations made in the report; however, they can hold a lot of weight, particularly in the interim proceedings.

I know from having practised in various cities in Australia that the cost of a private family report can vary significantly from state to state. Having said that, if you are paying privately, then it is likely to be a significant expense no matter where you live. One option to consider is to request that the court appoint a court-employed family consultant for an 's62G(2)' family report. This is when the court makes a 'section 62G(2) order' appointing a family consultant to prepare the report. The cost of that report is met by the court, which could save you thousands of dollars. The court will need to be satisfied that you and your ex-partner are not in a financial position to pay for a report. If your ex-partner can pay for a private report but you cannot, then consider a request that your ex-partner meet the full cost of any report.

 *Private family report or section 62G(2) report? If the court makes an order for a family consultant to prepare the report pursuant to section 62G(2), then you will not need to pay for the report.*

Independent children's lawyers

In a lot of the work that I do in my practice, I am appointed by the court to act as an independent children's lawyer (ICL). We were previously known as the *'child representative'*.

An ICL is appointed to represent the interests of a child rather than acting on their *instructions*. All ICLs must have been working in the Family Law jurisdiction and completed national ICL training. The appointment of an ICL is not automatic and the court will not make the order in all parenting matters. There are case law and guidelines setting out matters where it may be appropriate. To summarise, it may include matters where:

- There are allegations of child abuse
- There is intractable conflict
- There are allegations of alienation
- There are cultural or religious considerations
- There are issues of sexual preference
- There is family violence
- The child is of mature age
- There has been separation of siblings
- Both parties are self-represented

Where both parties are self-represented, there is a higher likelihood that an ICL will be appointed as most judges find the ICL very helpful in terms of information gathering, making submissions and progressing a matter. An ICL can help the court to fill the gaps that may be evident when one or both parties are self-represented.

ICLs are funded by state Legal Aid offices. Most parties who are employed are required to contribute towards the cost of ICLs; however, those costs are generally nominal in comparison to paying your own lawyer. Applications to waive fees can be made if you are in a position of financial hardship.

If you think an ICL will be beneficial in your parenting matter, then you can request that the court make an order for the appointment of an ICL either in your court documents or verbally. Consider whether they may be able to assist by gathering information, assessing evidence, speaking with school teachers and generally ensuring that the best interests of your child are at the forefront of the court proceedings. Remember that an ICL must act impartially; they are not appointed to represent you; however, they can be a means to support your position.

TIPS — *Consider asking for an order for the appointment of an independent children's lawyer if you are self-represented and feel that the ICL will be able to obtain information relevant to your matter.*

Ongoing negotiation and mediation

So, your matter has ended up in court. This does not mean that the negotiation stops! If at any time you feel as if there is scope to settle or further negotiate your parenting or property matter, then you should do so. Some clients are surprised when I tell them that we can continue to put forward offers of settlement and negotiation even though there are court proceedings. In some circumstances, this will be a waste of your time; however, if there is scope to resolve your matter, then I would encourage you to explore those options. Would an offer to settle be helpful? You should get some legal advice around whether to make those offers '*without prejudice*', so that they cannot be shown to the court, or whether to submit formally filed offers for property matters. Is an informal conference or mediation a good option? There is nothing precluding the parties from trying alternative resolution with a view to getting the matter out of court.

 *Just because your matter is in court does not mean that negotiation or other options to resolve the matter are out the window!*

Trial

Thankfully, the majority of matters do not reach trial. Generally speaking, when a matter is in trial, the parties are only allowed to rely on one standalone trial affidavit, which is filed late in the proceedings. If your matter is proceeding to trial and you are proceeding on a self-represented basis, then consider obtaining some unbundled legal services for fixed fees to prepare your trial documents. That way, you can ensure you have a good set of documents for the court to rely on.

If you'd like a detailed step-by-step guide to court proceedings (including information in relation to interim proceedings and trial), my firm offers an accurate, detailed and cost-effective online course, which you can find via www.familylawproject.com.au.

If you do have a lawyer (or are considering changing lawyers), then this is definitely a time to be discussing fixed-fee options for the preparation for trial.

If your matter proceeds, then consider whether you need both a solicitor and barrister present. If your solicitor limits their time at court, then that will potentially save you thousands of dollars. Also be mindful that barristers generally charge their fees on a daily basis or part thereof. If you can avoid your negotiations going over to another morning of trial, then you will also likely save thousands of dollars. I have unfortunately seen examples of barristers being keen to continue negotiations to the following morning of trial so that they can claim another full day of fees.

TIPS – GOING TO COURT:

- *Now that your matter is in court, obtain updated legal and procedural advice about what to expect during the court process, even if you've received legal advice previously.*
- *Remember that you may qualify for legal aid funding even if your application was previously rejected on the grounds of merit.*
- *It is worth spending time observing the court list of the judge that your matter is listed before.*
- *Put supports in place to help you deal with an ex-partner who uses money or persistence to drag out the case and also consider seeking cost orders in your favour.*
- *Be aware of 'hearing by ambush' and be as prepared as possible prior to each and every hearing. Try to pre-empt issues that may come up.*
- *Your registry may have a specialist property pool list for matters less than $500k.*
- *Consider attending court yourself to view and copy all of the material to reduce your legal fees if your lawyer has issued a subpoena.*

- *A s69ZW order may be more appropriate than a subpoena when you're seeking to obtain relevant information.*
- *You will not need to pay for a family report if the court makes an order for a family consultant to prepare the report pursuant to section 62G(2).*
- *If you are self-represented, consider asking for an order for the appointment of an independent children's lawyer.*
- *Just because your matter is in court does not mean the negotiation has to stop!*

Bonus Tips

THE TIPS BELOW DO NOT EXACTLY FIT UNDER THE TOPICS WE'VE covered in this book, but they may be really valuable for you, so I have included them here for you to keep in mind.

Superannuation

Contact your superannuation trustee. Whom have you nominated as a beneficiary? Many of us nominate a beneficiary with our trustee many years prior to separation. There is a good chance that your ex-partner is listed as your nominated beneficiary and the fact of your separation or divorce does not override that direction. It is a simple enquiry to make and it is not difficult to nominate a fresh beneficiary. Also check any life insurance policy and make updates accordingly.

 *Make the phone call to your superannuation trustee and immediately update your nominated beneficiary.*

Your will

Never had a will? Oh dear!

You need to seriously consider updating your will – or have a will drafted if you do not currently have one.

Separation itself does not rescind your will. If you were married, then divorce may revoke your will; however, your estate is still left with uncertainty. You want to avoid having your estate distributed under the laws of intestacy as opposed to your express wishes. Intestacy laws may have your ex-partner nominated as an executor and/or beneficiary. You need to update your will to ensure that you have nominated the beneficiaries you want to receive your estate. I suspect it is not your ex-partner! You want to ensure that the executor of your estate is also someone nominated by you. Again, I suspect you do not want your ex-partner controlling your estate upon your death.

You should also turn your mind to nominating guardians for any children.

You're not going to like this paragraph. Although I have provided a lot of cost-saving tips in this book, cutting corners with your will is not recommended. Please do not purchase a DIY will kit. Each state has very strict requirements in relation to the preparation of wills. There is so much room for error and if your will does not follow the strict requirements, it may ultimately cause more work for your executor upon your death. It will probably cost your family money, as a lawyer will likely be needed to file additional affidavit material with your probate application to explain any errors. In short, spending a few hundred dollars on a professionally drafted will is money well spent.

 *Do not try to save money when drafting your updated will. Your will needs to be updated upon separation but please avoid DIY wills. Preparation of a legally binding will is one of the best cost-saving measures you can take at this time to protect your interests. If you would like a free e-book on the importance of updating your estate when you separate, please feel free to email my office (lawyers@familylawproject.com.au).*

Power of guardianship & power of attorney

If you have recently separated, then estate planning is likely the last thing on your mind. Or at least something that you think you will deal with later. But updating your will and also your other estate documents is one of the first things you should do.

Power of attorney and power of guardianship documents have different names in each state, but the idea behind the documents is the same. A will is a document that comes into effect after your death. Power of attorney and power of guardianship documents are in place while you are alive and set out what is to happen in the event that you do not have capacity.

A power of attorney document sets out the persons that you nominate to make legal and financial decisions for you in the event that you suffer incapacity. You want to ensure that you are choosing who will be in charge of your financial affairs in the event of serious injury or an unexpected medical event that leaves you without capacity. The document will enable your trusted appointed attorney to do all sorts of practical things, such as accessing your bank account and paying bills and also making larger transactions such as the sale of real estate. It is important to update this document to ensure that your ex-partner is not involved with any of those decisions.

Updating your power of guardianship (or advanced care directives) also ensures that your ex-partner is excluded from making medical and dental decisions for you in the event that you no longer have capacity (perhaps you are in ICU, on life support, have been in a car crash, have lost mental capacity and so on). This document will ensure that you are appointing the person that you trust to make these decisions for you.

Update your power of guardianship and power of attorney. Updating both of these documents will help to exclude your ex-partner and also provide you with peace of mind that your loved ones have been appointed to manage your financial and medical affairs if you are not able to.

New relationships

Have you re-partnered? Did you just laugh out loud and think that's the last thing on your mind right now?! Believe it or not, it is possible to find love again!

If you have re-partnered, you are likely to have some reservations in terms of protecting your financial interests. There are some simple things to consider.

You may want to:

- Update your will (again!)

- Consider a binding financial agreement to protect your assets (a 'pre-nuptial' agreement). I could write a book on this topic alone – it's complex!

- Be mindful of the two-year rule for de facto relationships – is your new relationship soon to be subject to the protections and obligations of that state?

- Be mindful of buying property in joint names.

- Not register your relationship unless it is in your financial advantage to do so.

- Keep your finances separate if possible.

- Cross your fingers! (Just kidding!)

Seriously, though, I think it is the family lawyer in me that has seen the worst of the worst and causes me to raise this caution.

I recently had a client who resolved his matrimonial property settlement only to move in with his new partner and share finances – before he knew it, they had been living together for two years. Then they separated. He had hardly finished the first property settlement and this was devastating for him!

I would hate for you to have gone through one of the most difficult periods in your life only to have that repeated, albeit in a different way. The reality is that we do not always get the fairytale ending that we are anticipating.

 *Consider protecting your position in any new relationship, given your separation experience.*

Family violence

I have not discussed family violence at length in this book, but that is not because I am minimising the impact that family violence can play in a separation and Family Law matter. If you were the victim of family violence, you will require a number of tools to support you through your separation and the Family Law process.

 *If you have experienced family violence, seek legal representation.*

Given your situation, it will always be preferable for you to have legal representation to strongly advocate for you and to protect you from coercive and controlling behaviour and from any power imbalance. There are a number of family violence legal services who offer advice and representation for victims of family violence and I have included links to these services in the resources section of this book. These services will also be able to provide warm referrals to different counselling and non-legal support services, which are likely to be critical supports for you through your separation journey and beyond.

Support for men

It would also be remiss of me not to mention the difficulties that men face during their separation, particularly around the lack of specific service providers in the Family Law space. Men are overrepresented in suicide rates in Australia. According to Parents Beyond Breakup (PBB), approximately ten to eleven men will commit suicide in Australia each week due to separation issues. My view is that there does not appear to be the same level of Family Law support available to men that we see for women.

The reality is that men and women cope differently with their relationship breakdown. PBB provided input for my book *Separate Ways* and indicated that they were of the view that men in particular can become suicidal due to 'situational stress' arising from custody matters, the breakdown of a relationship and the loss of the family home. Some of the most common feelings experienced by people who PBB assists are isolation and hopelessness, as many people feel there is no solution to what they are going through. Organisations such as PBB and Dads in Distress understand the value of men sitting with other men, telling their stories and hearing each other's stories. Men get together as equals with their peers, shoulder to shoulder, and share their separation stories.

 *Recognise the lack of Family Law support for men and seek support relevant to your situation.*

Mental health

There is an increased risk of acute distress and depression for both men and women following separation. Separation and divorce are commonly cited as a 'life event' that can trigger depression. Unfortunately, many people are ashamed to seek help or even acknowledge that they're struggling. But this can make it much, much worse. In the wake of a separation, it's critical that you prioritise your mental health.

Your general practitioner can write a mental health care plan for you, with a referral to a psychologist. The plan provides a number of free or subsidised sessions with that psychologist each year. A psychologist or counsellor can offer advice, guidance and coping mechanisms.

In addition to seeing a counsellor or psychologist, there may also be various support groups or specific counselling services that are relevant to you. Examples are domestic violence counselling or drug and alcohol counselling.

 *Prioritise your mental health. Turn to the resources section of this book for details of organisations you may find helpful.*

Final Thoughts

I SUGGEST THAT, FROM TIME TO TIME, YOU FLIP BACK THROUGH this book to remind yourself of the various cost-saving tips that I have given you. Not all tips are likely to be relevant to you the first time you read this book; however, I suspect that most of the tips will be relevant at some point throughout the course of your Family Law journey.

This book has attempted to arm you with knowledge and information to avoid legal overwhelm, but it is likely that you will benefit from further information and resources, particularly if you are navigating your Family Law matter on a self-represented basis. I have included information on helpful legal resources at the end of the book. Many of the resources you can access are free or low cost. My law firm attempts to make Family Law as accessible as possible and we provide free resources on our social media pages and website, free webinars (minus the legalese!), free-first-call telephone advice meetings and also an online Family Law course. Head to our website for further details and bookings (www.familylawproject.com.au).

No matter what your Family Law matter costs you financially, you should always factor in your emotional wellbeing and self-care when making decisions and weigh up what is important to you.

This book has really focused on the technical side of Family Law and separation, with lots of practical and financial tips to help you on your journey. But there will always be an emotional cost when navigating your separation and Family Law matter, no matter the circumstances of your separation or how amicable the separation has been.

I have included in this book a reference to my previous book, *Separate Ways: Surviving Post-Separation Grief, the Stress of Divorce or Separation*, and the Family Law Process. It's a deep dive into understanding the stages of grief and loss in the context of separation and a strong resource that provides you with advice and strategies to survive this period, including input from many mental health professionals. I have provided information about further mental health support at the end of this book and encourage you to reach out.

I wish you the very best as you navigate your Family Law journey.

Caveat

LIKE ALL GOOD LAWYERS, I STARTED THE BOOK WITH A standard 'caveat', stating that the contents of this book are not intended as legal advice, as every matter is unique. *This is a reminder that this book is not intended to be a substitute for professional legal advice.* Also remember that while I speak of the Australian Family Law system, Western Australian residents are still dealt with pursuant to their own state legislation and state Family Court.

Please feel free to contact my office to discuss your specific matter.

The Family Law Project

The Family Law Project is a progressive and innovative specialist Family Law firm aiming to break down legalese and make Family Law services more accessible. They have a strong commitment to educating their clients and guiding them through their Family Law journey.

To find out more about The Family Law Project, access their online Family Law courses or book a free initial meeting with a lawyer, please visit:

www.familylawproject.com.au

Helpful resources

LIFELINE

lifeline.org.au | 13 11 14
24-hour crisis support and suicide prevention services

1800 RESPECT – NATIONAL DOMESTIC FAMILY VIOLENCE COUNSELLING SERVICE

1800respect.org.au

Telephone and online support and referrals for victims of family violence. 1800RESPECT is a good starting point to link in with support services that are relevant to your needs.

ANGLICARE AUSTRALIA

Anglicare offers parenting courses such as 'Kids Are First' and 'Mums and Dads Forever Program'. Each state offers different courses and support, so search for Anglicare in your particular state.

BEYOND BLUE

beyondblue.org.au
1300 22 4636

Mental wellbeing assistance, including 24/7 telephone support and online support.

CHILD SUPPORT (SERVICES AUSTRALIA)
csa.gov.au
Information for parents about child support payments and assessments.

CIRCLE OF SECURITY INTERNATIONAL
circleofsecurityinternational.com
Resources for parents, including Circle of Security Parenting program.

COMMUNITY LEGAL CENTRES AUSTRALIA
clcs.org.au
Provides links to hundreds of community legal centres across Australia with individual listings for each state.

FAMILY LAW COURTS AND NATIONAL ENQUIRY CENTRE
familycourt.gov.au
Forms, information about the court and filing of documents. Also provides link to the *Family Law Act 1975*. Cannot provide legal advice.

FAMILY RELATIONSHIP CENTRES
familyrelationships.gov.au
Post separation support and family dispute resolution (mediation) services.

MENSLINE AUSTRALIA
mensline.org.au
1300 78 99 78
MensLine is a free telephone and online counselling service for men, including relationship breakdown and parenting support.

NATIONAL LEGAL AID
nationallegalaid.org
Each state administers legal aid to assist clients who cannot afford legal representation. You can search the National Legal Aid website to find the legal aid commission in your state.

PARENTS BEYOND BREAKUP & DADS IN DISTRESS
parentsbeyondbreakup.com
1300 853 437
Parents Beyond Breakup is a specialised suicide prevention charity, with the tagline 'Keeping parents alive, and in their kids' lives'. Services include online support and face-to-face support groups around Australia. Dads in Distress specialises in supporting men.

RELATIONSHIPS AUSTRALIA
relationships.org.au
Relationships Australia offers support for families, including relationship advice, family dispute resolution (mediation) and parenting/education programs.

REDBOOK
redbook.com.au
Low-cost valuations of motor vehicles.

Glossary: Guide to legal terms

Affidavit

A formal written statement of facts which sets out the evidence that someone is relying on. The affidavit may set out the evidence of a party to the proceedings or of a witness. The document is sworn or affirmed in the presence of a Justice of the Peace or a lawyer. The affidavit is then filed with the court and served on the other party. In the Family Law Courts, an affidavit is the main way that the parties present their evidence.

Barrister

Barristers are lawyers. A barrister is a type of lawyer who specialises in court litigation. Barristers are required to study a '*bar*' course and undergo training. Each state in Australia differs slightly in terms of the role, but generally speaking, a barrister will require a solicitor to provide them with instructions to act for a client (i.e. the barrister works for the solicitor). Most trials will be conducted by a barrister. If you need a barrister in your matter, then you should ensure that the barrister engaged is one who specialises in Family Law.

Chronology document

A chronology document sets out a list of key and critical events in date order. It may include parenting and property issues (or both). Think of it as a summary document which enables your lawyer or someone that you are talking to about your matter to get a better understanding of the significant issues. The idea of the document is to be precise and include all of the essential information. Include all key dates such as dates of relationships/marriages, birth dates of people involved, including children, dates of any family violence, dates that you have spent with children (if contested), dates of purchase or disposal of significant property, dates of inheritances and so on. You should also include the 'source' of the information so that it can be identified. A 'source' may be things such as a police report number, reference to an SMS message or email and so on. It can be a good idea to prepare this document before your first meeting with a lawyer or mediator. It is often described as a 'living' document in that you will likely continue to add to the document after separation.

Conciliation conference
A conciliation conference is a court-ordered conference facilitated by a registrar of the court in an attempt to resolve your property and financial issues. If parties are legally represented, then their lawyer attends the conference with them. Parties who are self-represented attend by themselves. There will be orders made in anticipation of the conciliation conference which must be complied with beforehand to ensure the best opportunity to resolve matters at the conference. Each state differs, but generally speaking there will be an ongoing requirement for discovery and document exchange prior to a conference. The court will likely also order that any property in dispute be valued. A balance sheet or financial questionnaire may need to be prepared and exchanged. You will need to check the court orders to see what specific orders have been made in your matter. If an agreement is reached during the conference, then the registrar can make legally binding orders setting out the agreement for property division and you may not need to go back to court. Generally,

two hours are set aside for a conciliation conference, but you should allow further time in case the registrar allows continued negotiations.

Consent orders
Consent orders set out the agreement by the parties for either their property or parenting matter (or both). It is a way to formalise your matter and obtain a legally binding court order without the need to go to court. When an agreement is reached, consent minutes of order are drawn up, which set out the agreement reached in a legally binding way. Agreements in relation to property division usually require the assistance of a lawyer to ensure they are drafted correctly. The agreement, along with supporting documents, is submitted to the court without the need to attend a court hearing. The documents are instead considered by a registrar of the court and if they approve the agreement, it has the effect of a binding court order. Once the consent minutes are approved, both parties must comply with them and they can only be changed by further agreement between the parties or with an application to the court. That said, it can be very difficult to change orders once they are in place.

Cost order
Generally speaking, in Family Law matters, each party is responsible to pay their own legal costs. It is known as a 'no cost jurisdiction'. There are some exemptions and the court does have discretion to make an order for one party to pay all or part of the other party's costs (known as 'party-party costs'). This will usually require a written or oral application and the costs payable are usually set out in the Scale of Costs. When considering whether it is appropriate to make a cost

order, the court must consider section 117(2) of the *Family Law Act*. That section includes considerations such as the financial circumstances of each party, the conduct of each party, whether one party deliberately delayed proceedings, whether costs were incurred because of the failure of a party to follow court orders (i.e. breach of orders), written offers to settle the matter and whether one party has been wholly unsuccessful with their application.

Discovery
There is an ongoing obligation in property matters to disclose relevant financial and property documents. The aim of the disclosure process is to keep matters out of court or, if they are in court, to ensure that the parties are focusing on genuine issues and attempting to settle their matter. The rules in relation to disclosure require parties to disclose all information that may be relevant, such as financial resources, assets, income, debt and superannuation. Documents will include things such as bank statements, superannuation statements, and appraisals and valuations of businesses and other property. Each side is entitled to ask for specific documents that are relevant. If you fail to disclose relevant information, then it can have a negative effect and if you are in court, then cost orders may be made against you.

Divorce
A divorce is the legal process for terminating your marriage. A divorce order is obtained from the Family Law Courts and the application before the court only deals with the issue of formally terminating the marriage. A divorce does not set out arrangements for your matrimonial property division or financial

dispute, nor does it deal with arrangements for any children.

Family consultant

Family consultants assist families who are in the Family Law Court system to resolve their parenting disputes. They are usually psychologists or social workers who specialise in working with separated families and with children. Family consultants may be ordered by the court to become involved in a parenting dispute at various stages. They may be involved early in the proceedings to meet with the parties (and possibly the children) to help identify the immediate needs of the family and provide a short memorandum to the court with recommendations. If proceedings are unlikely to resolve the issue, then they may be ordered to prepare a family report. The family report process involves having access to all court documents that have been filed and meeting with the parties and children over a longer period. If a child is of an age and maturity where it is appropriate, then the consultant will ascertain the child's views. A lengthy report (generally twenty to thirty pages) is provided to the judge and will include recommendations for the living arrangements for the children. Other recommendations may be made to improve communication between the parties or to address any parenting concerns. It is important to know that all dealings with a family consultant are *not* confidential. The judge is not bound by any recommendations made in a memorandum or a family report but will certainly take any recommendations into consideration.

Family Dispute Resolution

Family Dispute Resolution (FDR) is a type of mediation to assist separated families to reach agreement in relation to their parenting or financial matters. There is the expectation that people will not apply to the Family Law Courts for parenting matters unless they have first attempted to resolve their matter through FDR. There are some exceptions, such as urgent matters, matters involving family violence or where a child is at risk. There are various types of FDR, including lawyer-assisted FDR. Most states in Australia have Legal Aid offices that provide lawyer-assisted FDR for those who qualify for legal aid. Other commonly used FDR services for those without lawyers include places like the Family Relationships Centres, Centacare and Relationships Australia. Always ensure that the practitioner facilitating the FDR is a qualified practitioner and able to issue 'section 60I certificates' in the event that no agreement is reached. This certificate acts as evidence that you attempted FDR and it will generally enable you to initiate court proceedings, if appropriate.

Independent children's lawyer

An independent children's lawyer (ICL) is a lawyer appointed by the court to represent children and to ensure that their best interest and welfare is paramount. The ICL represents the child's interests and not their direct instructions. ICLs are not appointed in every parenting matter and the court must first be satisfied that certain criteria are met, such as: allegations of child abuse, an intractable conflict, parental alienation, antisocial behaviour of parties, family violence, serious mental illness, separation of siblings and so on. The court follows certain guidelines and each matter differs. Any party can apply to the court to appoint an ICL or the judicial officer can make the order even if nobody is asking for the order. The ICL must form an independent view based on the evidence available and must act in the best interest of the child. An ICL is not the child's legal representative and is not obliged to act on the child's instructions because, sometimes, the ICL will form the view that what the child wants is not in their best interest. The parties are to contribute towards the cost of the ICL unless they are in receipt of legal aid or are able to establish that they are in a position of financial hardship.

Leave of the court
The expression 'leave' of the court means to obtain permission or an order from the court enabling you to do something. For example, you may need to be granted leave before you file certain court documents. Another example is that you may need leave to be allowed to proceed with a property application that is out of time.

Minute of orders & consent minutes
A minute of order is a document which sets out the orders that you are seeking to be made by the court in the event there is no agreement. A *consent* minute of order is a document which outlines the terms of the agreement reached between the parties and acts as a proposal that the parties jointly put to the court to request that orders be made in those terms. Consent minutes of order can be presented to the court at any stage during court proceedings. Consent minutes are also required in circumstances where the parties do not have court proceedings but have submitted paperwork requesting that the court make orders (without having to go to court).

Orders
Court orders are the decisions made by the judicial officers of the court. Orders can be made in relation to both property and parenting matters. Orders are legally binding and all parties

must follow and comply with the orders.

Parenting plan

A parenting plan is a written and signed document which sets out the agreement for living and parenting arrangements for children. It is less formal than orders and is not legally enforceable if either party breaches the agreement. The benefit of a parenting plan is that it is generally a low-cost option for parents and it can work particularly well for parties whose separation has been amicable. Parents can draw up the plans themselves or use a lawyer or mediation service to assist them to draft the agreement. Although a parenting plan is not legally enforceable, if it is signed by both parties and dated, then it can be shown to the court if it needs updating or if one party is not complying with the agreement.

Registrar

A registrar is an officer of the court who has limited decision-making powers compared to a judge. Registrars generally hear all divorce applications, facilitate conciliation conferences and sit in procedural hearings.

Service of documents

The court needs to be satisfied that all parties to the proceedings are aware of the proceedings and that they have received documents. Proof of service needs to be filed with the court and that is usually through an Affidavit of Service. There are different ways to serve certain documents. The Federal Circuit Court website provides a good explanation of the various types and also has a pro forma affidavit available (www.federalcircuitcourt.gov.au).

Services Australia

Services Australia is the government department which accesses and collects child support payments. Many people still refer to the service as the 'Child Support Agency', which actually ceased to exist in 2011 when replaced with Services Australia.

Solicitor

Solicitors are lawyers. Many simply refer to themselves as 'lawyers'. In some states solicitors are not recognised as being able to advocate in court. Generally speaking, solicitors will be your first port of call to provide legal advice and guidance. It is the solicitor's role to provide you with legal advice, draft letters and documents, liaise with the other party (or their lawyer, if they have one) and assist you to resolve your matter. If your matter needs to go to court, then the solicitor will provide advice about whether a barrister is required for court advocacy.

Subpoena

A subpoena is a legal document issued by a party in court proceedings directing a person or an organisation to either attend court to give evidence or to produce documents for the court. Subpoenas are issued when this is the only way that the information can be obtained. The person or organisation is compelled to comply unless there is a legal reason for an objection. The types of subpoena commonly used in Family Law matters include: medical records, bank or accounting records, employment records, police records and child protection records.

Trial

The trial is the final hearing day or days that have been allocated to a matter. All Family Law proceedings need a date to be finalised and the trial is where a judge will hear all evidence and then make a decision. It is noteworthy that the majority of matters do not reach the final trial stage and will settle by agreement at an earlier date during the proceedings. Parties usually have barristers represent them at trial and any witnesses will also need to attend. The parties and witnesses will be cross-examined as part of the testing of the evidence to assist the judge to make a final decision.

Waiver of court fees

If you can establish financial hardship or if you are in receipt of a Centrelink benefit, then you will likely qualify to waive certain fees. The application to waive the fees can be obtained directly from the court.

Acknowledgements

I HAVE BEEN KEEPING MENTAL NOTES OF DIRTY LAWYER TACTICS in my mind for almost twenty years! I started jotting down tips back in 2017 and spent five days writing in Bangkok, but then put the manuscript to the side to write *Separate Ways: Surviving Post-Separation Grief, the Stress of Divorce or Separation, and the Family Law Process*. I do get distracted easily.

The manuscript had been put to the side, but in late 2020 my business structure changed and I formed a new business partnership with Elham Rabbah, who is now a director of The Family Law Project.

Elham has been fully supportive and encouraged the manuscript to come to life so that *Secrets of a Divorce Lawyer* can help thousands of people who have separated.

Thank you, Elham, for having confidence in me and *almost* never standing in the way of any of my crazy ideas.

About the author

SHAYA LEWIS-DERMODY IS A SPECIALIST FAMILY LAWYER WITH almost twenty years' experience. She has worked with thousands of Family Law clients across Australia and New Zealand. She is also regularly appointed by the court to act as an independent children's lawyer in complex custody disputes.

Shaya is the author of *Separate Ways: Surviving Post-Separation Grief, the Stress of Divorce or Separation*, and the Family Law Process, which was named a Finalist in the Australian Business Book of the Year in 2020.

In 2019 and 2020, Shaya was a finalist in the national Women in Law Awards, in the categories Thought Leader of the Year and Innovator of the Year. She has also been voted by her peers as a Doyle's Guide leading lawyer.

Shaya is the founding director of The Family Law Project, which is a socially responsible and progressive Family Law firm, with a focus on access to justice. Shaya started the firm because she was frustrated over the lack of quality and accessible Family Law services and recognised a gap in the market for fixed-fee lawyers.

Shaya is regularly featured as a thought leader in her field. She has conducted media interviews with ABC Radio, *The Saturday Paper*, *Domain* and many more.

To find out more about The Family Law Project, access their online Family Law courses or book a free initial meeting with a lawyer, please visit: www.familylawproject.com.au.

www.ingramcontent.com/pod-product-compliance
Lightning Source LLC
Chambersburg PA
CBHW071428070526
44578CB00001B/35